To my husband Allan, whose love lights the way.

Acknowledgements

I wish to thank the following people for their support and encouragement in the writing of this book: the Mt. Lebanon Public Library, the Children's Book Writing Group of Mt. Lebanon, my Foxland Drive neighbors Cory, Scott, and Erin Polena, Carol Baicker-Mckee, Jeff Cordell, and Andrea Perry, and my children Brian Joseph, Aliza, Debbie, Darren, and Matt.

This book would not have been possible without the talent and dedication of the following people at Williamson Publishing: Susan and Jack Williamson, Jennifer Ingersoll, Judy Raven, June Roelle, Jennifer Adkisson, and the creative talent of Joseph Lee of Joseph Lee Design and illustrator, Michael Kline.

Williamson Books
by Judy Press
The Little Hands® Art Book
The Big Fun Craft Book
Vroom! Vroom!

Copyright © 1997 by Judy Press

All rights reserved.

No portion of this book may be reproduced mechanically, electronically, on the Internet, or by any other means including photocopying without written permission of the publisher. Little Hands®, Kids Can!®, Tales Alive®, and Kaleidoscope Kids® are registered trademarks of Williamson Publishing Company.

Library of Congress
Cataloging-in-Publication Data

Press, Judy, 1944-
    Vroom! Vroom!: making 'dozers, 'copters, trucks & more/Judy Press.
            p.   cm. — (Williamson kids can! book)
    Includes index.
    Summary: Provides instructions for using milk cartons, egg cartons, and other materials to make such vehicles as cars, buses, sailboats, and more. Includes related projects to help the reader appreciate each vehicle.
    ISBN: 1-885593-04-X
    1. Motor vehicles—Juvenile literature. 1. Handicraft—Juvenile literature. [1. Vehicles. 2. Handicraft.] I. Title.
II. Series.
Tl147.P74   1997
745.5—dc20   96-27204
                                  CIP
                                  AC

Cover design: TREZZO-BRAREN STUDIO
Interior design: JOSEPH LEE DESIGN, INC.
Illustrations: MICHAEL KLINE
Printing: CAPITAL CITY PRESS

Williamson Publishing Co.
P.O. Box 185
Charlotte, Vermont 05445
1-800-234-8791

Manufactured in the United States of America

10 9 8 7 6 5 4 3 2 1

Notice: The information contained in this book is true, complete, and accurate to the best of our knowledge. All recommendations and suggestions are made without any guarantees on the part of the author or Williamson Publishing. The author and publisher disclaim all liability incurred in connection with the use of this information.

A Williamson *Kids Can!*® Book

Vroom! Vroom!

Making 'dozers, 'copters, trucks & more

by
Judy Press

Illustrations by Michael Kline

Williamson Publishing
Charlotte, Vermont

Table of Contents

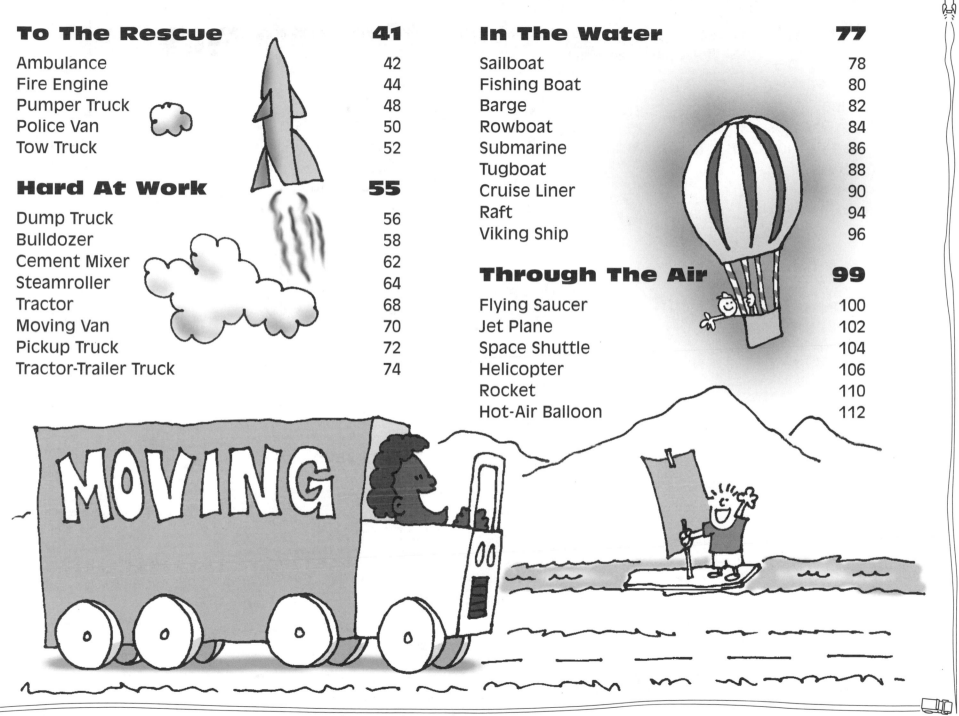

Fasten Your Seat Belts!

Is your bike your favorite way to get from here to there? Or, maybe you dream of flying to the moon some day aboard a space shuttle. Some people like to visit fire stations to see the long hook-and-ladder trucks; others think a construction site full of bulldozers and cement mixers is the greatest. Perhaps you prefer to dream of floating above the trees in a hot-air balloon. Whatever your favorite mode of transportation, get ready to blast off to a good time!

Ready, Set, Go!

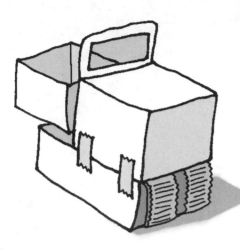

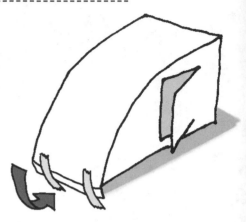

You are in the driver's seat when it comes to making and decorating any of the projects in this book. You can choose to make these vehicles go as far, as high, or as deep as you like. They can be decorated in bright colors, shiny foil, or left with the words "milk" or "spaghetti" on the sides of the boxes. Each craft is sturdy enough to be played with in your bed (or under it), or you can take it along with you to be enjoyed in a tent, a sandbox, a park, or, in some cases, even your bathtub.

There's no doubt about it; some of the projects are more complicated to make than others. There are wheel symbols next to each project: one wheel is the least complicated and will probably take the least amount of time, two wheels can be a little more challenging, and three wheels might take some figuring out and a good imagination. You know what you feel like doing and how much time you have. Maybe you can work on making a more challenging three-wheel project with someone else.

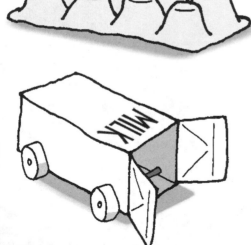

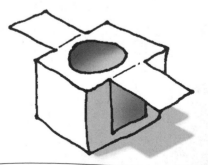

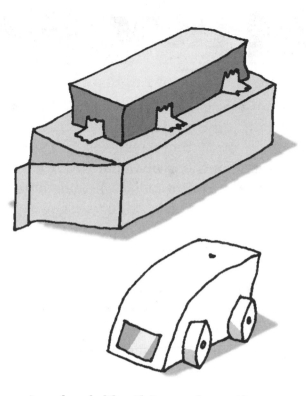

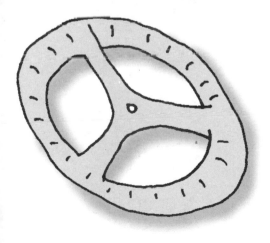

Sometimes in a book like this — where there are instructions about how to do something like attaching wheels — it seems that there are a lot of directions. If you feel that way, then I have a suggestion. Gather together the items in the materials list for a project you want to make (substituting if you are missing some things on the list). Then, think about what it is you want to make. Pick up the materials, turning them over, manipulating them, and looking at them from different directions. Look at the "exploded-view" illustrations. Then, just start putting the pieces together the way you want. There is no right or wrong way — *there is only your way!* The directions are there to help you get started. Use them every step of the way or don't use them at all. And remember, the most important thing you can bring to every project in this book is your imagination.

Safety First

Please observe these safety measures when doing art and crafts. They are really important.

Keep art and craft supplies away from young children. Remember that younger kids like to put things in their mouths and can pull sharp objects off tables. These projects use supplies that may be dangerous to toddlers. Finished projects should not be given to anyone younger than 4 years old.

Craft knife, scissors, pointed tool: When using anything sharp, please ask for a grown-up's help. If you are permitted to use these sharp objects alone, then always work on a hard, flat surface. Do not walk around or run while carrying these tools. Cutting cardboard is particularly difficult, so please ask for help (a sharp tool works better than a dull tool).

Use proper ventilation. Paints, paste, and glue should only be used in a well-ventilated room. In the winter, be sure to crack open a window or door.

Ask for help. You know the rules in your home or school. If a craft uses something that you are not supposed to touch, or if you are having difficulty cutting something, please ask for grown-up help. Thank you.

Recycle Alert

The great thing about most of the vehicles in this book is that you can make them from things that might otherwise be thrown away. So, start saving them now — in your room, in your house, and in school.

Milk cartons:
  half-gallon (1.89 l)
  quart (946 ml)
  pint (473 ml)
  half-pint (236 ml)

Pasta box (with cellophane window): 1 lb (454 g)

Sturdy paper plates, bowls, and cups

Egg cartons

Grocery trays from fruits or vegetables (no meat trays)

Cardboard paper towel and toilet tissue tubes

Cardboard cereal boxes

Recycled aluminum foil

Yogurt containers

6-pack dessert cups

Plastic barrel-shaped juice containers

Plastic berry baskets

Wooden ice-cream spoons

Popsicle sticks

Push-Up® and Rocket® pop sticks and disks (found in supermarket freezer case)

Drinking straws

Plastic wrap (clear or tinted)

Cardboard toothpaste boxes

Shirt cardboard

Cardboard cartons

Shoe boxes

Peanut packing material

Paper cups (to recycle, rinse thoroughly)

Craft Supplies

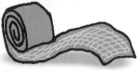

Scissors (for grown-up use only, unless you have permission)
Child safety scissors: a good pair
Pointed tool: nail, butter knife, tines of a fork
White craft glue
Markers
Tape (clear mailing and colors)
Stapler
Construction paper
Sticky-back Velcro®
Paper fasteners
Pipe cleaners
Pom-poms
Wiggly eyes
Paintbrush
Poster paint

And We're Off!

I hope you have fun making and playing with these vehicles, along with constructing towns and cities, highways and train tracks, lift-off stations and boat docks. Let your imagination go in new directions as you think about creating a new vehicle for the 21st century. Enjoy the ride, fasten your seat belt, watch the speed limit, and away you go!

Vroom! Vroom!

Basic Carton Construction

There are lots of things
you may want to know;
Gather your supplies—
Get ready, set, go!

Cutout Windows

Here's what you need

- Milk carton (any size)
- Ballpoint pen
- Nail or pointed tool
- Scissors

Here's what you do

❶ Rinse, dry, and open spout on the milk carton. Use a ballpoint pen to draw on windows.

❷ Use the pointed tool to pierce the center of the window and cut out with scissors.

OPEN →

MILK

Glued-On Windows

Here's what you need

- Milk carton (any size)
- Construction paper
- White craft glue
- Pencil
- Scissors

Here's what you do

❶ Use the pencil to draw the shape of windows onto construction paper.

❷ Cut out windows. Glue onto milk cartons.

Cab with Windshield

This is the basic cab without wheels added.

Here's what you need

- Milk carton (any size)
- Scissors
- Clear or tinted plastic wrap (optional)

Here's what you do

❶ Rinse, dry, and open spout on milk carton. Cut away 3 flaps from spout end of carton.

❷ Cut out the center of the remaining flap for a windshield. Tape plastic wrap across windshield.

Fixed Wheels

Fixed wheels are lots of fun and easy to make with handy supplies. You can have lots of fun pushing a vehicle along, even if the wheels don't spin.

Here's what you need

- Milk carton (any size)
- Heavy paper cup
- Paper fasteners
- Scissors
- Nail or pointed tool

Here's what you do

❶ Use the nail to poke holes in the sides of milk carton where wheels will be attached.

❷ Cut down the side of the paper cup and then cut around the bottom for a wheel. (The wheel is the bottom of the cup.)

❸ Attach wheel to carton with a paper fastener.

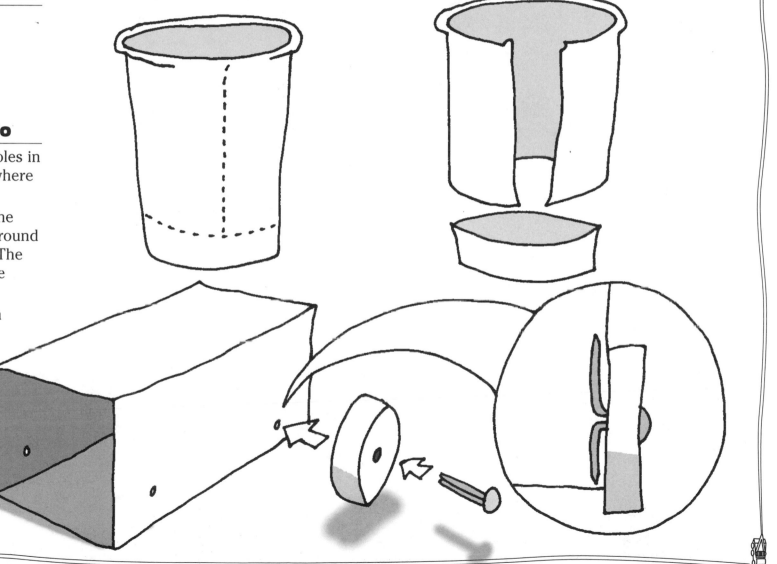

Rotating Wheels

Here's what you need

- 2 Push-Up® pops or 2 Rocket® pops (stick and disk)
- Milk carton
- Nail or pointed tool

Here's what you do

1 Use the nail to poke a hole in opposite sides of the milk carton where the wheels will be attached.

2 Press 1 Push-Up® or Rocket® pop disk onto its stick. Push through 1 hole and out the other. Attach second disk onto stick for wheels and axle.

Note: Tape 2 Push-Up® or Rocket® pop sticks together if a longer axle is needed.

NOW TRY THIS

☻ **For a burst of color on your bicycle wheels, weave strips of ribbon or crepe paper between the spokes.**

IN THE BEGINNING

The first wheels were solid discs made either from single pieces of wood or from 3 planks laid side to side, fastened together, and then cut into a disc shape

Basic Boat

This provides the basis for many of the boats you will make.

Here's what you need

- Milk carton (any size)
- Stapler
- Scissors

Here's what you do

❶ Rinse, dry, and open the spout end on the milk carton. Cut the carton in half vertically (the long way).

❷ Reform the remaining spout and staple closed for a boat.

IN THE BEGINNING

Fire and stone axes were used to hollow out tree trunks to make early boats called dugouts.

NOW TRY THIS

❶ Cut a triangle shape "boat" from an index card and float it in a bowl of water. Put a drop of liquid soap on your finger. Gently touch the water behind the boat with your finger. Watch the boat shoot forward.

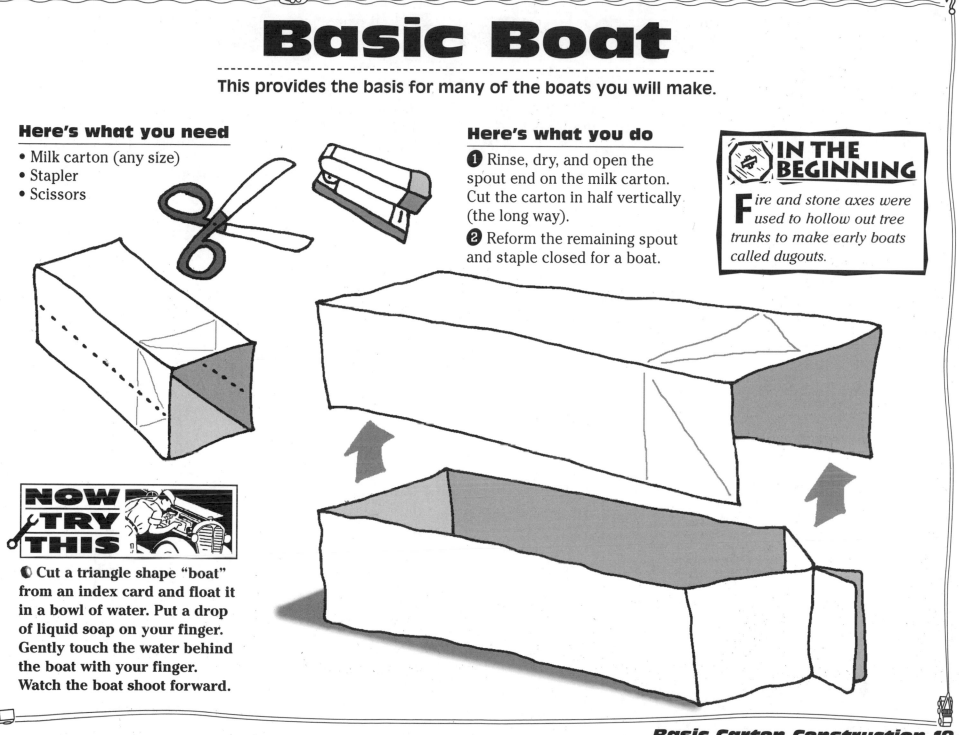

Painting Tips

Part of the fun in making things is that you can let your imagination run wild. Decorate your vehicles with paint, paper, stripes, sparkles, and stickers. It's up to you!

Here's what you need

- Milk carton
- Poster paint
- Liquid dishwashing detergent
- Empty yogurt container
- Paintbrush

Here's what you do

❶ Pour paint into the container and mix in a few drops of dishwashing detergent.

❷ Brush paint onto cardboard carton and allow to dry completely.

Helpful Hints:

1. Darker colors will cover print on cartons better than lighter shades.

2. Or, wrap cartons in white paper before painting for total coverage.

3. Do not paint cartons that go into water.

Note: To remove writing from a milk carton, ask a grown-up to spray the carton with Formula 409™ (Caution is advised when using this product near young children.) Allow a minute before rubbing with steel wool.

Vroom! Vroom!

Away We Go!

"How much longer? Are we there?"
These things you want to know,
It's so hard to sit and wait
To get where you must go.

School Bus

Here comes the yellow school bus
rolling down the street,
At the bus stop children wait
to board and take a seat!

Here's what you need

- Half-gallon (1.89 l) milk carton
- Egg carton
- Tape
- 2 sets wheels (page 17 or 18)
- Scissors

Here's what you do

❶ Rinse, dry, and open spout of milk carton. Lay carton on its side. Cut down 2 edges of top side for a roof flap. Cut windows in sides of carton and spout.

❷ Put 8 sections of egg carton into milk carton for passenger seats.

← tape closed

3 Attach wheels. Tape spout end closed. Tuck roof flap into carton for a bus.

BUS

IN THE BEGINNING

Two brothers, Frank and William Fageol, designed and built the first real American motor bus. In 1920, there were only 60 motor buses operating in the whole United States.

NOW TRY THIS

◐ Draw a picture of a bus driver and glue it to the front of the milk carton's roof flap. Then, make peanut passengers (page 116) and put them in the seats.

◐ Practice safety rules for boarding and exiting a school bus.

◐ Teach yourself or teach some younger children to sing "The Wheels on the Bus Go Round and Round."

Car

Turn the key in your play car,
flip on the radio,
Grab hold of the steering wheel,
step on the gas and go!

Here's what you need

- Egg carton lid
- Pasta box
- 2 sets wheels (page 17 or 18)
- Tape
- Scissors

Here's what you do

❶ Cut the lid into 2 pieces, 3" (7.5 cm) and 4" (10 cm). Cut out the hump in center of lid. Cut wheel wells in lid pieces, and a U-shape from end of longer piece.

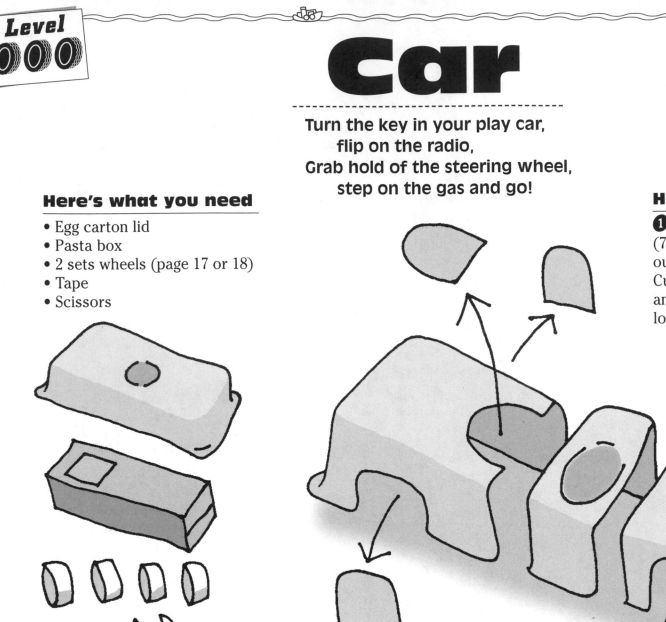

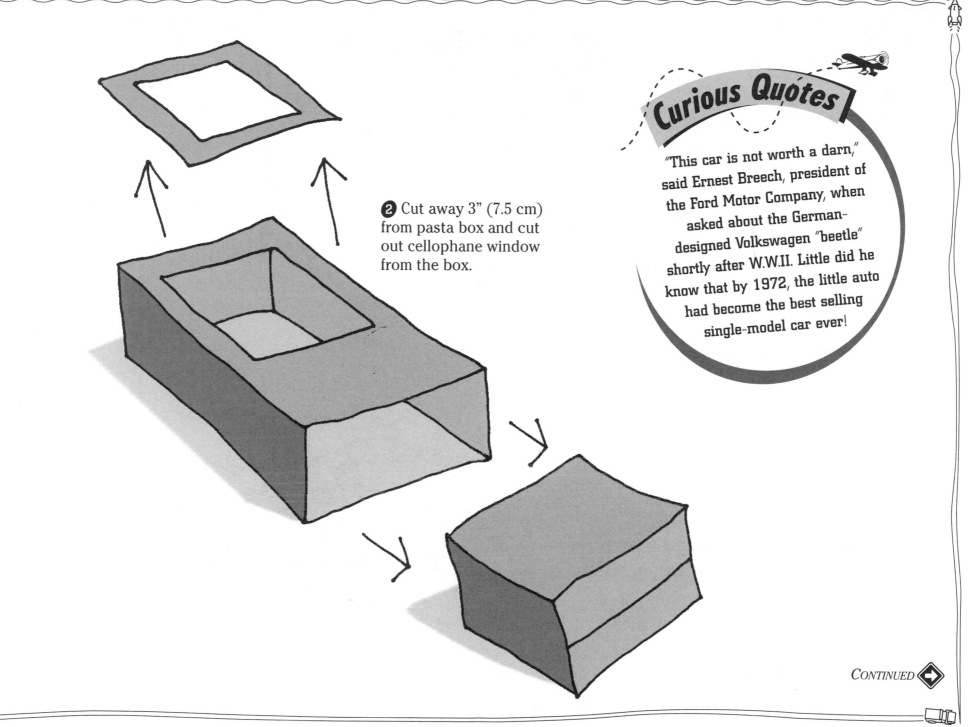

2 Cut away 3" (7.5 cm) from pasta box and cut out cellophane window from the box.

CONTINUED ▶

Curious Quotes

"This car is not worth a darn," said Ernest Breech, president of the Ford Motor Company, when asked about the German-designed Volkswagen "beetle" shortly after W.W.II. Little did he know that by 1972, the little auto had become the best selling single-model car ever!

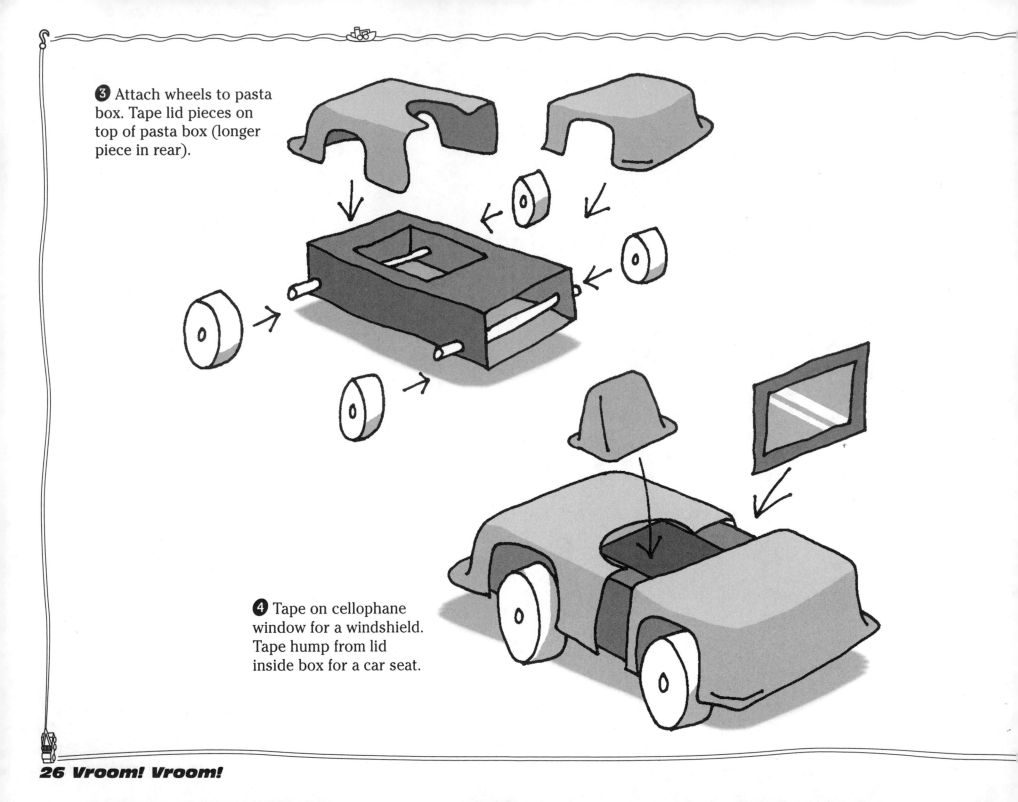

3 Attach wheels to pasta box. Tape lid pieces on top of pasta box (longer piece in rear).

4 Tape on cellophane window for a windshield. Tape hump from lid inside box for a car seat.

NOW TRY THIS

◐ Play "The Roadside Alphabet Game." Look at signs along the road to see if you can find, in sequence, each letter of the alphabet. Airport, Boston, Curve Ahead...

◐ Play a car color game. The first one to count ten cars of the same color wins.

Double-Decker Bus

A double-decker bus ride
will take you through the town,
There's so much that you can see
when you're up looking down!

BOTTOM HALF

Here's what you need

- 2 half-gallon (1.89 l) milk cartons
- 2 egg cartons
- Tape
- 2 sets wheels (page 17 or 18)
- Scissors

Here's what you do

❶ Rinse, dry, and open spout on milk carton. Cut 8 sections from each egg carton. Cut out windows on sides of both milk cartons. On 1 carton, cut windows in the spout.

FAST FACTS

In London, England, the red double-decker buses are a familiar sight, carrying passengers throughout the central section of the city.

2 Put egg carton sections into milk cartons. Tape spout flaps flat on carton without spout windows.

3 Attach wheels to bottom carton. Re-form spout with window and tape closed. Tape cartons together on top of each other.

NOW TRY THIS

◐ Many double-decker buses are used for sight-seeing. What sights would you show a visitor to your city or town?

◐ Draw a double-decker bus on shirt cardboard. Then, cut out the bus and cut out windows. Glue photos of family and friends in windows for a great frame.

◐ Read the book, *A Witch Got On At Paddington Station* by Dyan Sheldon. What country do you think Paddington Station is in?

Mini-Van

A van takes workers to their jobs,
and swim teams to the pool,
It makes deliveries around town,
and carries students to school!

Here's what you need

- Quart (1.89 l) milk carton
- Tape
- 2 sets wheels (page 17 or 18)
- Scissors

Here's what you do

1 Rinse, dry, and open spout of milk carton. Cut away 3 spout sides from carton. Cut half-way into carton along both sides of the remaining spout flap.

2 Cut windows in front and a door in the side of the carton. Bend flap down and then follow curve and cut away corners of carton.

3 Tape down carton flap and attach wheels for mini-van.

FAST FACTS

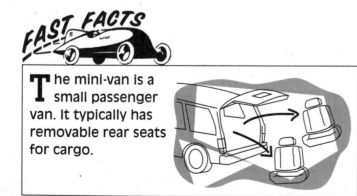

The mini-van is a small passenger van. It typically has removable rear seats for cargo.

NOW TRY THIS

🌑 Cut out pictures of mini-vans from old magazines and paste them onto construction paper for a collage.

🌑 Count how many mini-vans you see in 30 minutes.

🌑 Name everything you would pack in a mini-van if you were taking a trip to the beach or across the country.

High-Speed Train

You can sit down on a train,
or hold onto a strap,
You can talk or read a book,
or even take a nap!

Here's what you need

- 3 quart (946 ml) milk cartons
- Tape
- Sticky-back Velcro®
- White craft glue
- Pasta wheels
- Scissors

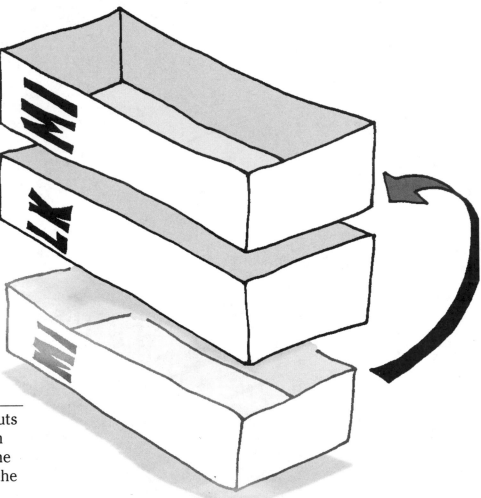

Here's what you do

❶ Rinse, dry, and open spouts of milk cartons. Cut 1 carton in half the long way. Tape one half upside-down on top of the other for a coal car.

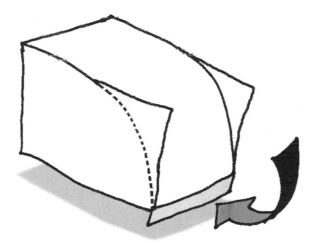

FAST FACTS

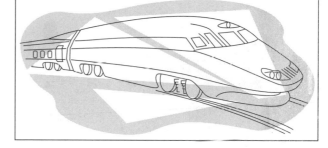

In Japan, bullet trains carry 200 million passengers a year at speeds of 130 miles (210 kilometers) an hour. In France, the bullet train, known as the T.G.V., reaches speeds of 223 miles (360 kilometers) an hour. The fastest train in the United States is the Amtrak Metroliner, which speeds along at 125 miles (202 kilometers) an hour between Washington, D.C. and New York City.

❷ Cut away 3 spout flaps from second carton. Cut half-way into carton along both sides of remaining flap. Bend flap down, then follow curve and cut away side corners of carton.

❸ Cut a windshield in front and side of carton. Tape down for a locomotive.

CONTINUED ➡

4 Cut windows in third carton and tape down spout flaps for a passenger car.

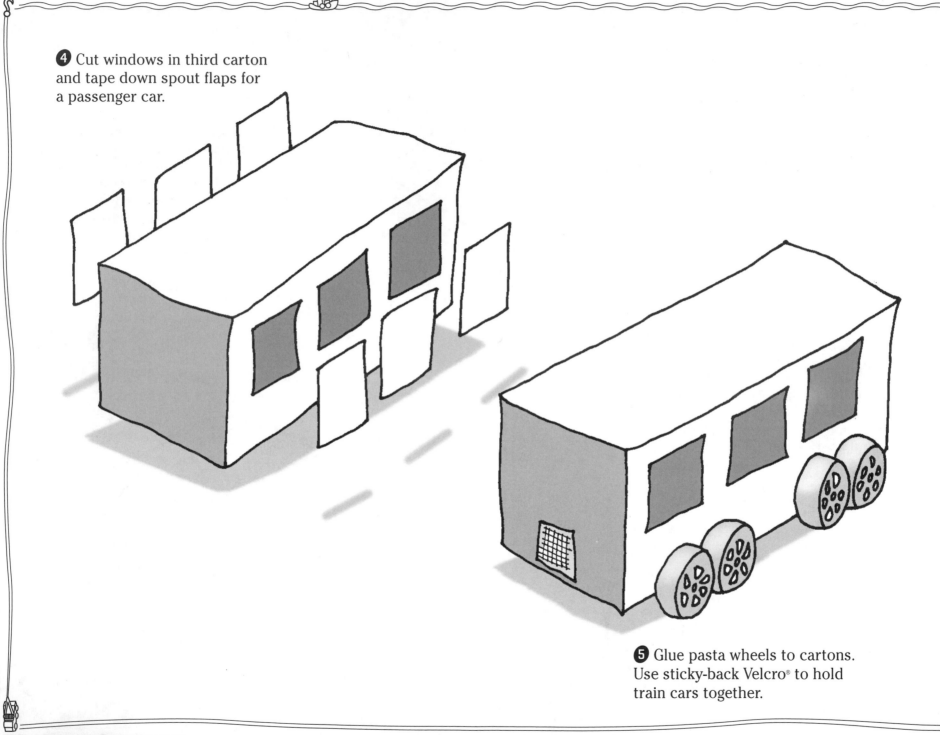

5 Glue pasta wheels to cartons. Use sticky-back Velcro® to hold train cars together.

ON THE JOB!

Conductor's ticket book

Cut shirt cardboard into two 4" x 7" (10 cm x 17.5 cm) rectangles. Cut sheets of white paper the same size. Place paper between cardboard and staple along the outside edge for a ticket book.

Race Car

Race cars roar around the track,
it's what they really need,
They can pass all other cars
when they pick up speed!

Here's what you need

- Half-pint (236 ml) milk carton
- Quart (946 ml) milk carton
- Fixed and rotating wheels, 1 pair each (pages 17 and 18)
- Shirt cardboard
- Tape
- Scissors

Here's what you do

❶ Rinse, dry, and open spout on milk cartons. Cut away spout flaps of both cartons. Lay the quart carton on its side and cut an opening in top. Put the half-pint carton inside.

❷ Cut triangles half-way into sides of quart carton, then tape flaps together. Cut 2 large wheels from cardboard.

❸ Attach rotating wheels to front of carton. Put cardboard wheels over top of fixed wheels and attach to back of carton with fasteners.

Checkered racing flag

Cut a flag from black construction paper. Make horizontal slits in flag that come short of the edge. Cut white paper in thin strips and weave into black flag. Trim edges and tape to hold. Wrap a paper towel tube in foil and tape on flag.

❍ Use bright-colored stickers to decorate your race car. Strips of colored tape make great racing stripes.

❍ Paint a race track on a large piece of cardboard. Allow to dry completely; then take your race car out for a drive.

❍ Write a great saying for a bumper sticker. How about "I LOVE MY PET IGUANA" or "THIS CAR BREAKS FOR BEARS."

Camper

If you're going camping,
 bring a sleeping bag along,
Sit around the fire,
 tell stories, and sing camp songs!

Here's what you need

- Half-pint (236 ml) milk carton
- Pint (473 ml) milk carton
- Recycled aluminum foil
- Tape
- Sticky-back Velcro®
- 2 sets wheels (page 17 or 18)
- Scissors

IN THE BEGINNING

In the frontier days, Daniel Boone and other early scouts and frontiers people spent months in the wilderness, camping wherever night overtook them on the trail. They used to enter into the wilderness equipped only with a rifle, a hatchet, a bag of salt, the means to strike a fire, and sometimes a frying pan.

Here's what you do

❶ Rinse, dry, and open spout of milk cartons. Make a cab from the half-pint carton (page 16).

❷ Cut away 3 spout flaps from pint carton. Cut half-way into the carton along both sides of the remaining spout flap.

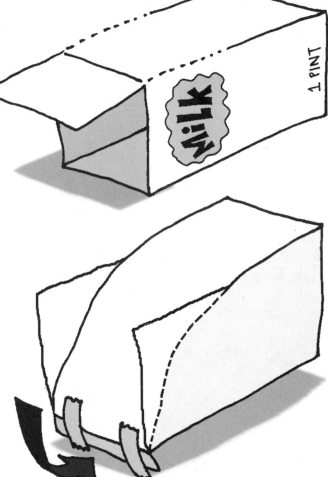

❸ Bend flap down; then follow curve and cut away side corners of carton and tape to hold.

❹ Cut a door in side of pint carton for camper.

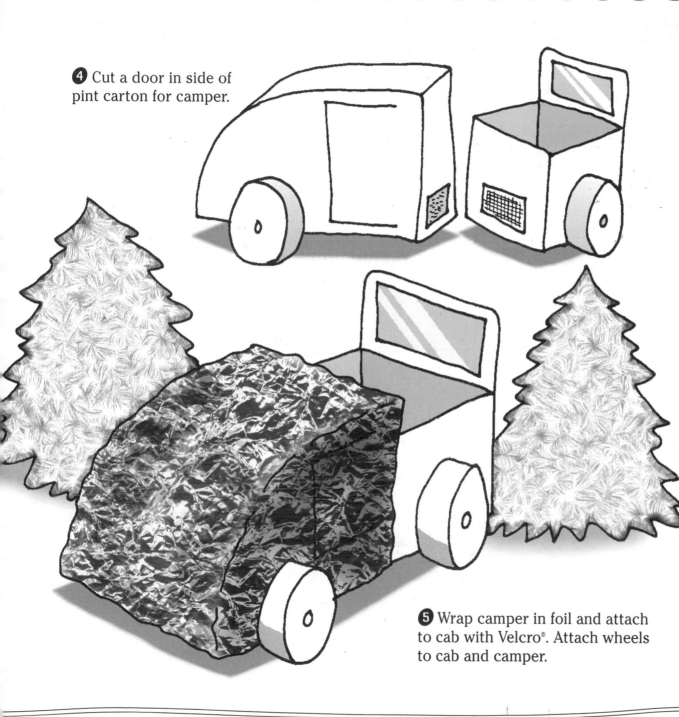

❺ Wrap camper in foil and attach to cab with Velcro®. Attach wheels to cab and camper.

NOW TRY THIS

◐ Sit indoors in a circle on blankets. Sing songs, tell stories, and eat on paper plates (don't forget the marshmallows).

◐ Learn to sing camping songs such as "She'll Be Coming 'Round The Mountain" and "White Coral Bells."

◐ Mix together equal amounts of unsalted nuts, dried fruit, chocolate chips, popcorn, and dry cereal for a batch of trail mix for your next hike or camping trip.

◐ Make a pitcher of Bug Juice — every camper's favorite punch. Mix together 1 envelope sugar-sweetened orange drink mix, 2 cups (500 ml) pineapple juice, 1/4 cup (50 ml) lemon juice (fresh or bottled), 1 quart (1 liter) cold water.

Moon Buggy

Here's what you need

- Pint (473 ml) milk carton
- Recycled aluminum foil
- 2 sets wheels (page 17 or 18)
- Straw and scrap paper
- Tape
- Scissors

Here's what you do

1 Rinse, dry, and open spout on milk carton. Cut away 3 spout flaps. Cut half-way into the carton along both sides of the remaining spout flap. Bend flap down; then follow curve and cut away side corners of carton. Cut a small hole in top of carton.

2 Wrap carton in foil. Attach wheels. Put straw in hole in carton, make flag, and tape to straw.

A visit to the planets is coming very soon. We will need a new buggy to drive across the moon!

IN THE BEGINNING

In December 1972, Apollo 17 astronauts drove a lunar roving vehicle on the surface of the moon. Besides carrying two people, it held film, a T.V. camera, special tools, and a communications unit for sending pictures back to Earth.

NOW TRY THIS

- Beginning on the first day of any month, draw the moon each night.

- Cut a moon shape from recycled aluminum foil. Paste the moon on dark blue or black paper and use chalk to draw a nighttime moonscape.

To The Rescue

When something unplanned happens,
it's hard to understand,
But there're so many people,
who'll lend a helping hand.

Ambulance

Sirens roar and red lights flash,
whether night or day,
When there's an emergency,
help is on the way!

Here's what you need

- Pint (473 ml) milk carton
- Half-pint (236 ml) milk carton
- 3 sets wheels (page 17 or 18)
- Sticky-back Velcro®
- Scissors
- Red gumdrop (optional)

Here's what you do

❶ Prepare cab from half-pint carton (page 16). Attach 1 set of wheels to cab.

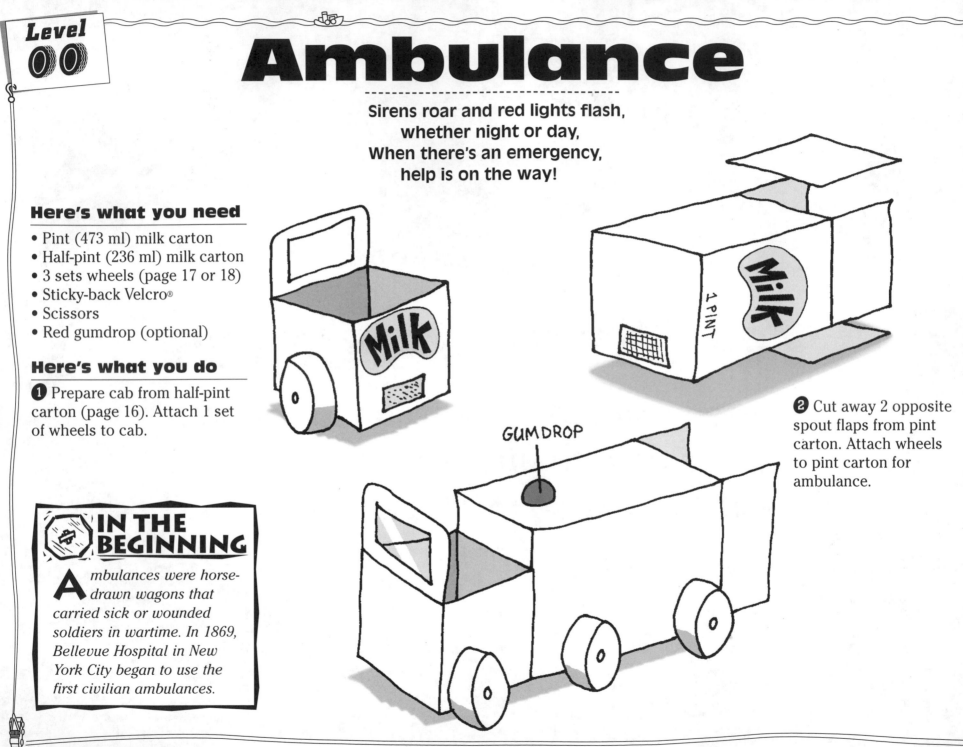

❷ Cut away 2 opposite spout flaps from pint carton. Attach wheels to pint carton for ambulance.

GUMDROP

IN THE BEGINNING

Ambulances were horse-drawn wagons that carried sick or wounded soldiers in wartime. In 1869, Bellevue Hospital in New York City began to use the first civilian ambulances.

Many ambulances have the word AMBULANCE (ECNALUBMA) or RESCUE (EUCSER) spelled backwards on the front of their vehicles. This is so the word will be spelled correctly when a car driver sees it in the rearview mirror. How do you spell your name backwards? (Hint: Hold your name up to a mirror.)

NOW TRY THIS

Put together a first-aid kit in a shoe box. Be sure to include gauze pads, tape, scissors, cotton balls, Band-Aids™, tweezers, and an ace bandage.

To make a stretcher for your ambulance, glue a piece of white paper between two Popsicle sticks. Make a wooden ice-cream spoon patient.

3 Use Velcro® to hold flaps closed and to attach ambulance to cab. Glue gumdrop on top for emergency light.

Fire Engine

Shiny fire engines
will soon be on their way,
Rush to put the fire out—
there's no time to delay!

GRAB YOUR BERRY BASKET. LET'S GO!

Here's what you need

- Quart (946 ml) milk carton
- Pint (473 ml) milk carton
- Half-pint (236 ml) carton
- Cardboard toothpaste box
- Plastic berry basket
- 4 paper fasteners
- Tape
- Sticky-back Velcro®
- 3 sets wheels (page 17 or 18)
- Scissors
- Red gumdrop (optional)

Here's what you do

❶ Rinse, dry, and open spout on milk cartons. Make cabs from pint and quart cartons (page 16).

❷ Cut away spout flaps from half-pint carton. Cut berry basket for ladders. Cut toothpaste box in half lengthwise.

3 Lay quart carton on its side and bend back windshield. Slide half-pint carton into opening. Attach 1 set wheels to pint cab and 2 sets wheels to quart carton. Use Velcro® to hold cartons together.

FAST FACTS

Fire fighters work in teams. They use walkie-talkies for communication, wear special clothing, and carry breathing apparatus on their backs.

CONTINUED ⬧

1 QUART

1 PINT

½ PINT

IN THE BEGINNING

In the early 1600s, American colonists used large leather buckets filled with water to fight fires. When a fire was discovered, the townspeople would bring their buckets and form tow lines between the fire and the nearest source of water. Buckets full of water would be passed up one line, the water thrown on the fire, and the buckets passed back down the other line to be refilled.

❹ Hang ladders on the half toothpaste box with fasteners; then tape box on top of quart carton. Glue on gumdrop for emergency light.

NOW TRY THIS

● Conduct a practice fire drill at home. Find two ways to leave your room and decide on an outdoor meeting place.

● Ask a grown-up to check the smoke alarms in your home and replace the batteries if necessary.

● Read *Firehouse* by Katherine K. Winkleman to learn more about fire fighters.

Pumper Truck

Pumper trucks hook hoses
to a hydrant's spout,
Then they spray some water
and put the fire out!

Here's what you need

- Pint (473 ml) milk carton
- Quart (946 ml) milk carton
- Paper fasteners
- 3 sets wheels (page 17 or 18)
- Yarn
- Sticky-back Velcro®
- Scissors
- Red gumdrop (optional)

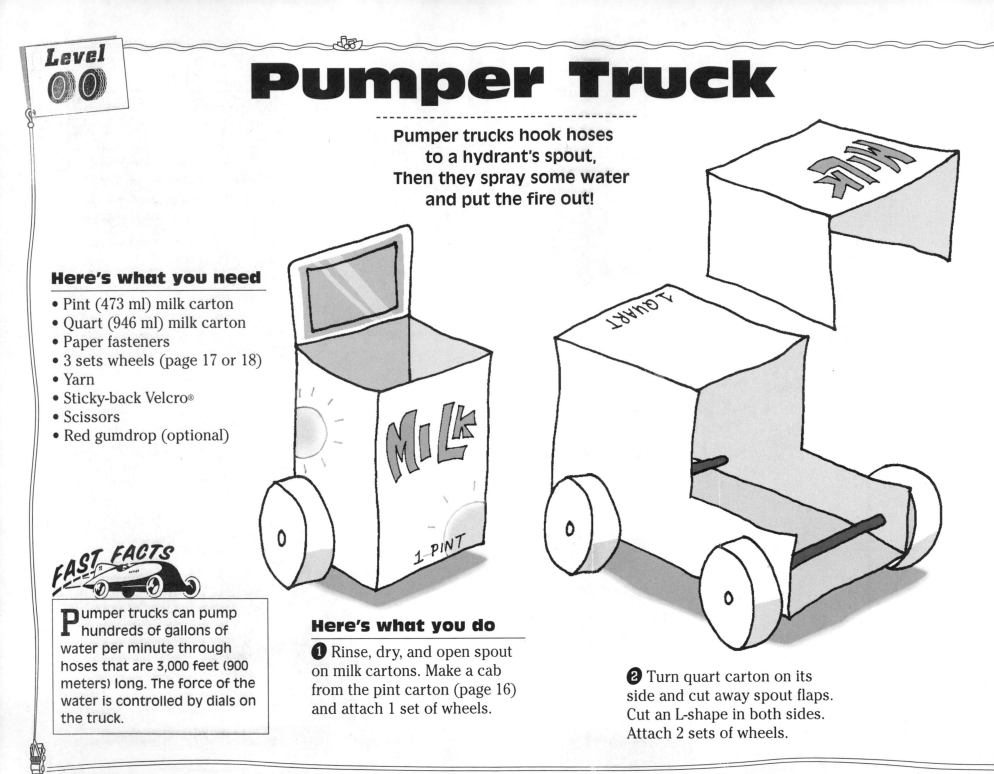

FAST FACTS

Pumper trucks can pump hundreds of gallons of water per minute through hoses that are 3,000 feet (900 meters) long. The force of the water is controlled by dials on the truck.

Here's what you do

❶ Rinse, dry, and open spout on milk cartons. Make a cab from the pint carton (page 16) and attach 1 set of wheels.

❷ Turn quart carton on its side and cut away spout flaps. Cut an L-shape in both sides. Attach 2 sets of wheels.

3 Use Velcro® to join cartons. Wrap yarn around fastener in side of carton for hose (store extra yarn inside carton). Glue gumdrop on top for emergency light.

NOW TRY THIS

❶ Pumper trucks hook their hoses up to fire hydrants. Look for the hydrants in your neighborhood.

❶ Pumper trucks sometimes use water from rivers or lakes to fight fires. To see how water is brought up from the river, put a straw in a glass of water and cover the top with your finger. Raise straw out of glass.

Police Van

Friendly police are special guests
who like to visit schools,
They talk about the job they do
and teach some safety rules!

Here's what you need

- Half-pint (236 ml) milk carton
- Pint (473 ml) milk carton
- Sticky-back Velcro®
- 3 sets wheels (see page 17 or 18)
- Scissors
- Red gumdrop (optional)

Here's what you do

1 Rinse, dry, and open spout on milk cartons. Make a cab from the half-pint carton (page 16) and attach 1 set wheels.

2 Cut away 2 opposite spout flaps from pint carton for a van. Attach 2 sets wheels to pint carton.

IN THE BEGINNING

A round 1928, in London, England, a man named Sir Robert Peel set up the first modern police force. The London police officers are called "Bobbies" because of Sir Robert.

3 Use Velcro® to attach cab to van and to close flaps. Glue gumdrop on top for emergency light.

ON THE JOB! Officer's badge

To make a badge you can wear, cut the shape of a badge from shirt cardboard. Squeeze a thin line of glue onto the cardboard in the shape of a number. Press string into glue and let dry. Wrap foil around badge and smooth over string. Tape pin to back of badge.

NOW TRY THIS

🔵 Teach someone younger than you the safety rules for bicycle riding. ALWAYS wear a helmet when you ride.

🔵 Look up the police emergency number and post it next to the telephone.

🔵 Read *Officer Buckle and Gloria* by Peggy Rathmann. In what ways do animals help people?

Tow Truck

When there's engine trouble
and your car gets stuck,
There's no need to worry—
Look! Here's the tow truck.

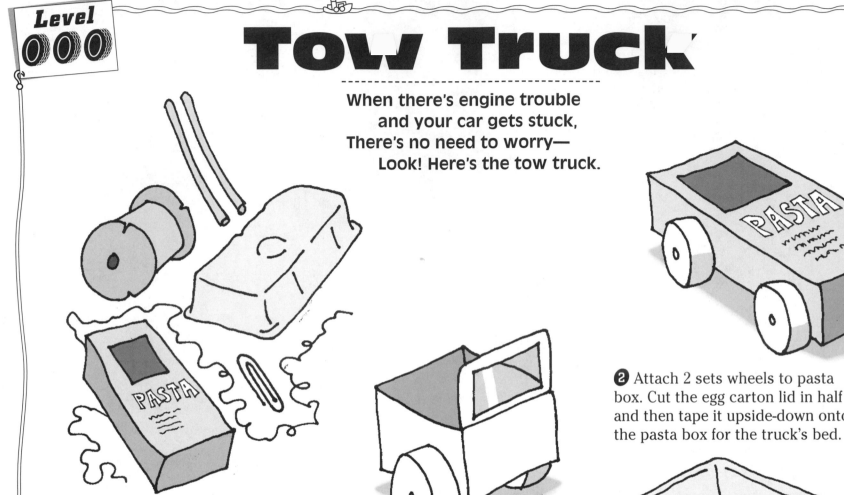

❷ Attach 2 sets wheels to pasta box. Cut the egg carton lid in half and then tape it upside-down onto the pasta box for the truck's bed.

Here's what you need

- Half-pint (236 ml) milk carton
- Pasta box
- 3 sets wheels (page 17 or 18)
- Empty thread spool
- 2 straws
- Egg carton lid
- Tape
- String and paper clip
- Scissors

Here's what you do

❶ Make a cab from the half-pint carton (page 16). Attach 1 set wheels.

❸ Wrap string around spool and thread through the straw. Tape straw to rear of truck bed. Put second straw into center of spool and through holes in sides of egg carton lid.

FAST FACTS

Sometimes called a "wrecker," the tow truck rescues cars. Tow trucks have strong cranes and chains to lift the end of a car. This makes it easier to pull a damaged car to the repair garage.

CONTINUED

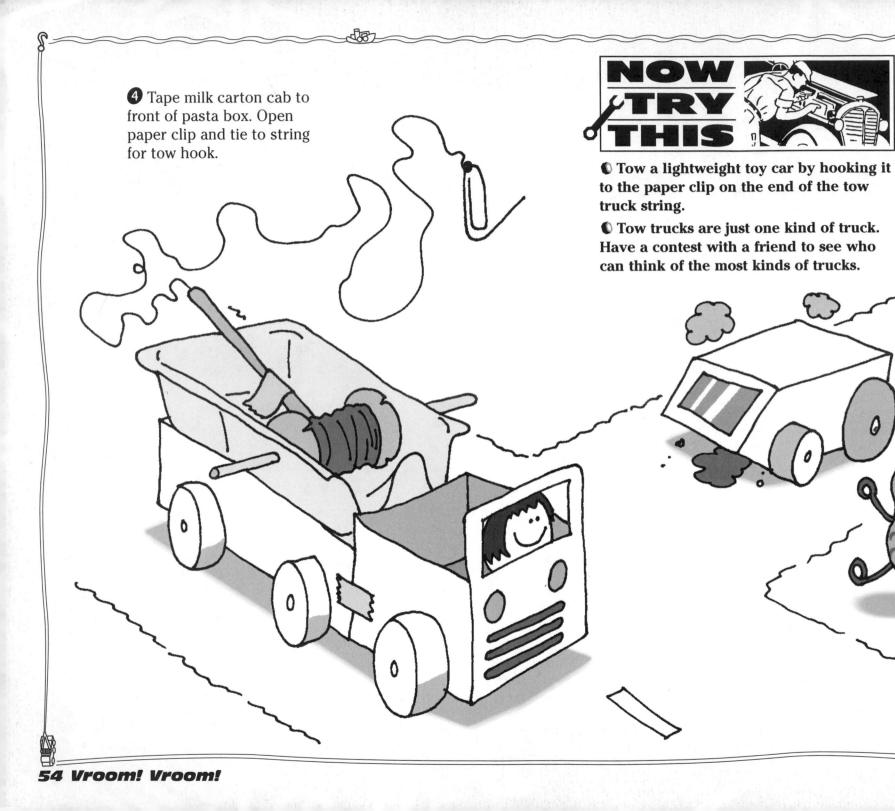

4 Tape milk carton cab to front of pasta box. Open paper clip and tie to string for tow hook.

NOW TRY THIS

◑ Tow a lightweight toy car by hooking it to the paper clip on the end of the tow truck string.

◑ Tow trucks are just one kind of truck. Have a contest with a friend to see who can think of the most kinds of trucks.

Vroom! Vroom!

Hard At Work

Rolling down the highway
are trucks that weigh a ton;
Workers in a hurry
to get their big jobs done!

Dump Truck

A dump truck's coming down the road
toward a building site,
First it tips and drops its load,
then it becomes upright!

Here's what you need

- Grocery store fruit tray with high sides
- Pasta box
- 2 strips shirt cardboard
- 6 paper fasteners
- Half-pint (236 ml) milk carton
- 3 sets fixed wheels (page 17)
- Sticky-back Velcro®
- Scissors

IN THE BEGINNING

*T*he first vehicles for carrying loose materials, such
as sand or coal, were flat-
bedded trucks with sides that
could be taken off or let down
on hinges. Workers used shov-
els to load and unload them.
It was not long before someone thought of tilting the body
so that the contents could be
tipped out. Now, the driver
operates a lever inside the
cab to unload the truck. The
box behind the cab tilts, and
the load is dumped out.

Here's what you do

❶ Make a cab from the half-
pint carton (page 16). Attach 1
set wheels.

❷ Cut the tray in half the long
way. Cut the pasta box the same
length as the tray. Attach the
front set of wheels to pasta box.

3 Overlap halves of tray and hold together with paper fasteners. Rest tray on pasta box; then use paper fasteners to attach strips of cardboard on sides of tray between the rear wheels and the pasta box so tray moves up and down. Attach the remaining wheels to rear of pasta box over the cardboard strip.

4 Attach cab to pasta box with Velcro®.

NOW TRY THIS

○ Fill your dump truck with beans or macaroni; then lift the dumper body to unload into a pan.

○ Ask a grown-up to take you to a construction site so you can see many kinds of trucks.

Bulldozer

Bulldozers do construction work,
they're like a giant cup;
First they dig way down underneath,
and then they scoop things up!

Here's what you need

- 2 pint (473 ml) milk cartons
- Half-pint (236 ml) milk carton
- Pasta box
- Shirt and corrugated cardboard
- 4 paper fasteners
- Tape
- Scissors

Here's what you do

❶ Rinse, dry, and open spouts on milk cartons. Make a cab from 1 pint carton (page 16). Then cut away spout flaps from half-pint carton.

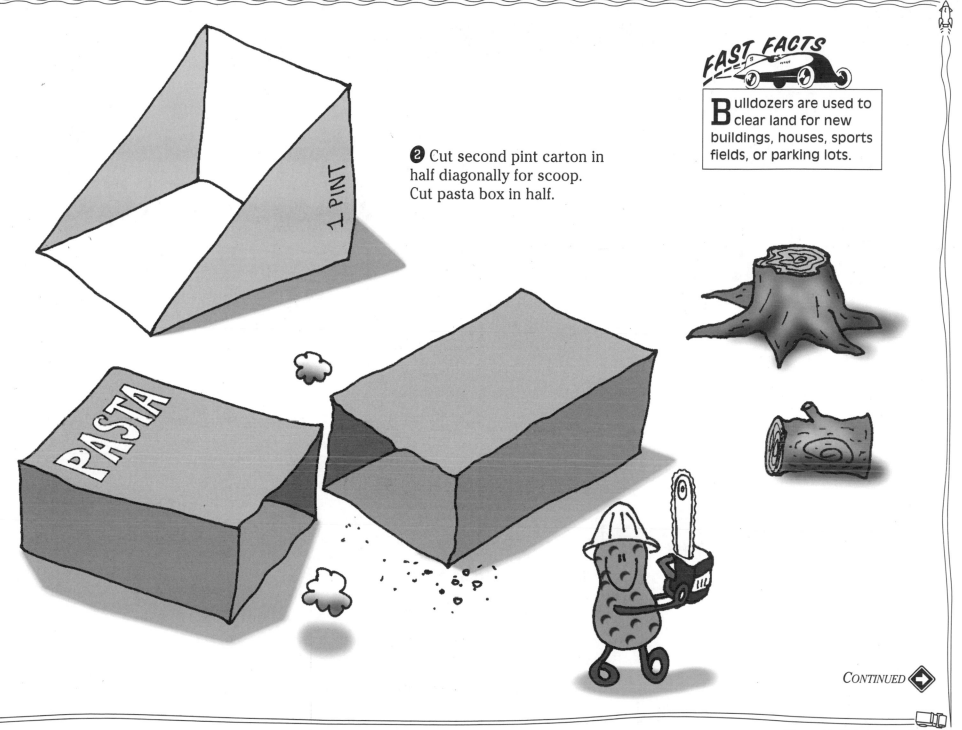

2 Cut second pint carton in half diagonally for scoop. Cut pasta box in half.

1 PINT

PASTA

CONTINUED ▶

FAST FACTS

Bulldozers are used to clear land for new buildings, houses, sports fields, or parking lots.

❸ Tape 2 strips of corrugated cardboard around pasta box.

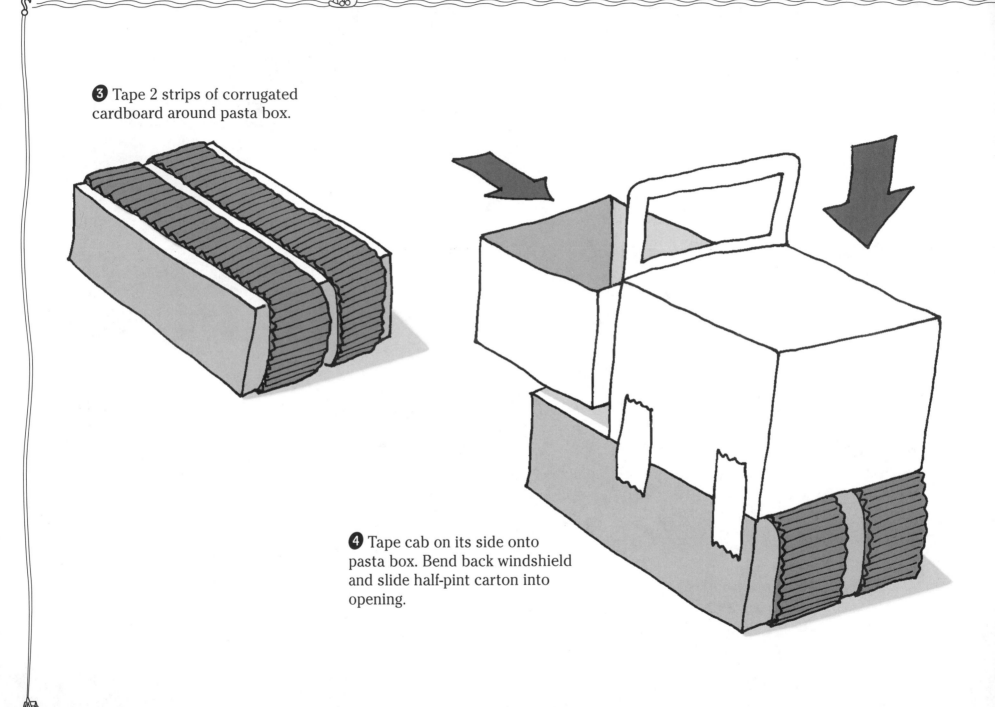

❹ Tape cab on its side onto pasta box. Bend back windshield and slide half-pint carton into opening.

5 Use paper fasteners to attach 2 strips of shirt cardboard to sides of pint cartons to raise and lower scoop.

NOW TRY THIS

◐ Put rice or beans on a cookie sheet and use your bulldozer to make big hills.

◐ Watch a bulldozer working on a construction site. Why do you think bulldozers work on tracks of steel instead of tires?

◐ Is *Mike Mulligan and His Steam Shovel* by Virginia Lee Burton one of your favorite books? If it is, then take it out to read again; if you've never read it, then borrow a copy from the library.

Cement Mixer

Cement trucks are like mixing bowls —
they twist and turn about,
By adding water, gravel, sand,
cement pours out the spout!

Here's what you need

- Quart (946 ml) milk carton
- Half-pint (236 ml) milk carton
- Plastic barrel-shaped juice bottle
- Pasta box
- Sticky-back Velcro®
- 3 sets wheels (page 17 or 18)
- Scissors

Here's what you do

❶ Rinse, dry, and open spout on milk cartons. Make a cab from half-pint carton (page 16). Attach 1 set wheels.

½ PINT

❷ Cut quart carton in half diagonally. Cut pasta box in half and cut away most of the box's top side. Attach 2 sets wheels.

PASTA

1 QUART

FAST FACTS

The drum of the cement mixer is filled with a mixture of cement, sand, gravel, and water. A motor turns the big tank over and over, like a spinning top on its side, to keep the cement from hardening.

3 Put quart carton into pasta box at an angle. Put juice bottle into quart carton. Now attach pasta box to cab with Velcro®.

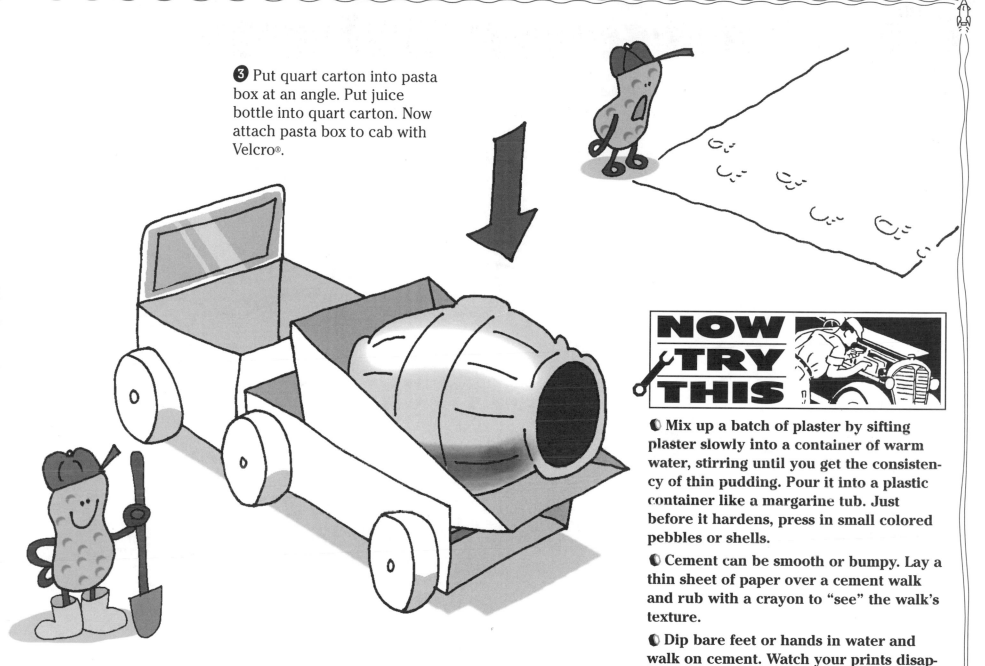

NOW TRY THIS

◐ Mix up a batch of plaster by sifting plaster slowly into a container of warm water, stirring until you get the consistency of thin pudding. Pour it into a plastic container like a margarine tub. Just before it hardens, press in small colored pebbles or shells.

◐ Cement can be smooth or bumpy. Lay a thin sheet of paper over a cement walk and rub with a crayon to "see" the walk's texture.

◐ Dip bare feet or hands in water and walk on cement. Watch your prints disappear in bright sunshine.

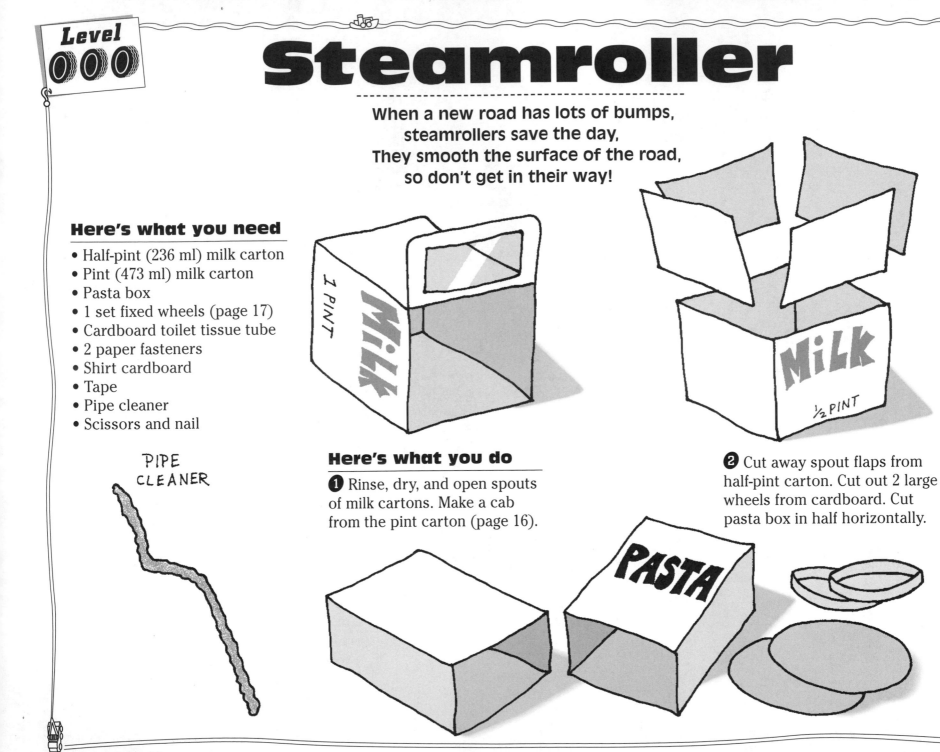

Level ⦿⦿⦿

Steamroller

When a new road has lots of bumps,
steamrollers save the day,
They smooth the surface of the road,
so don't get in their way!

Here's what you need

- Half-pint (236 ml) milk carton
- Pint (473 ml) milk carton
- Pasta box
- 1 set fixed wheels (page 17)
- Cardboard toilet tissue tube
- 2 paper fasteners
- Shirt cardboard
- Tape
- Pipe cleaner
- Scissors and nail

PIPE CLEANER

Here's what you do

❶ Rinse, dry, and open spouts of milk cartons. Make a cab from the pint carton (page 16).

❷ Cut away spout flaps from half-pint carton. Cut out 2 large wheels from cardboard. Cut pasta box in half horizontally.

1 PINT

MiLk

MiLk

½ PINT

PASTA

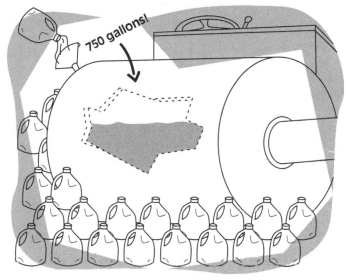

Asphalt is made of sand, gravel, and oil. The steamroller travels over the newly laid asphalt. The huge drum in front of the roller is filled with over 750 gallons (2812.5 l) of water, making the roller heavy enough to pack down the asphalt.

750 gallons!

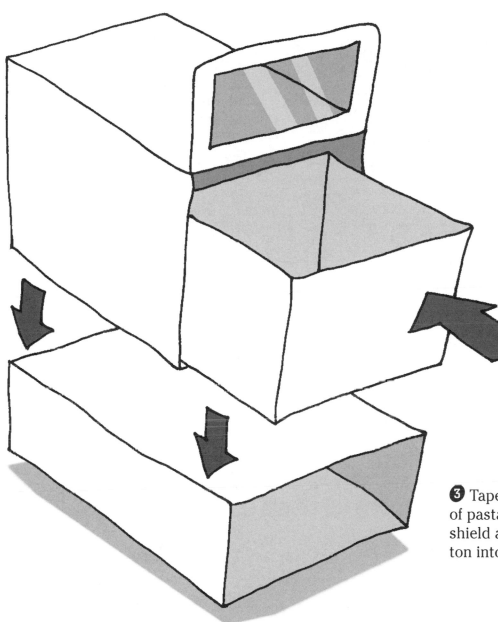

3 Tape cab on its side to top of pasta box. Bend back wind-shield and slide half-pint carton into opening.

CONTINUED ➡

4 Put fastener through cardboard wheels and fixed wheels before attaching to pasta box.

5 Punch small holes (with nail) in sides of half-pint carton.

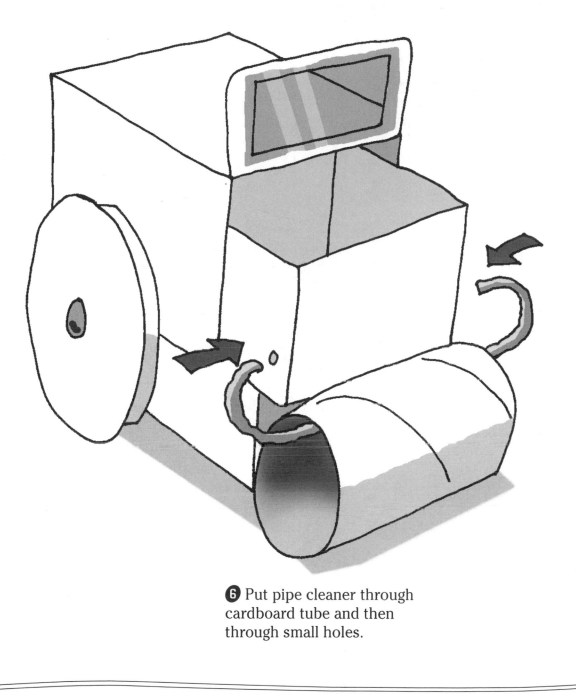

6 Put pipe cleaner through cardboard tube and then through small holes.

● Mix up a batch of play dough. Flatten it out using different utensils: a rock, a rolling pin, a jar filled with water, your hand, the back of a wooden spoon. Which way works best?

● Next time you make a trip to the store in a car, compare the different road surfaces such as newly laid, patched, potholed, and dirt. Which is bumpiest?

Tractor

**A tractor moves through the fields
to plow the earth in rows,
Once a seed is planted there,
the farmer hopes it grows!**

Here's what you need

- Half-pint (236 ml) milk carton
- Pint (473 ml) milk carton
- Pasta box
- Plastic berry basket
- 2 strips corrugated cardboard
- Tape
- Scissors

Here's what you do

1 Rinse, dry, and open spouts on milk cartons. Cut away the spout end, bottom, and 1 side of the pint carton. Cut half-pint carton in half diagonally. Cut pasta box in half horizontally.

IN THE BEGINNING

Not so long ago horses provided the pulling power for farmers. When more traction was needed, two, three, or more work horses were hitched together to do farm jobs like pulling plows, harvesting grain, and carrying crops to market.

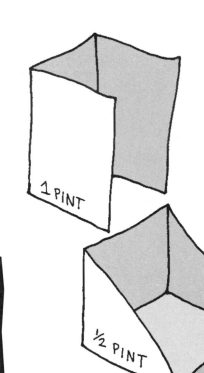

1 PINT

½ PINT

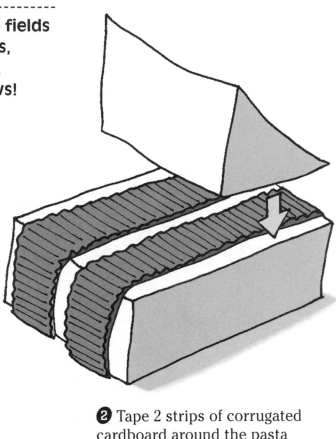

2 Tape 2 strips of corrugated cardboard around the pasta box. Then tape the half-pint carton on top.

PASTA

3 Fold the remaining strip from the pint carton in an arc over the pasta box and tape to hold. Cut bottom of berry basket to fit across front of arc for a grille.

FAST FACTS

A farmer pulls a plow behind his tractor, turning up the soil to make a soft bed for the seeds. The discs of the plow create rows, or furrows, as they rotate behind the moving tractor.

NOW TRY THIS

⚙ Traction, or pulling power, depends on surface conditions. Walk on loose, dry beach sand. Then, walk where the beach sand is moistened by waves. Which condition is easier to walk on?

⚙ Visit a working farm to see how the farmer uses a tractor to plant the crops.

⚙ Buy fresh produce such as beans, carrots, onions, and celery from a farm market. Then make a pot of vegetable soup.

Moving Van

On moving day they load your things
through van doors open wide,
The truck pulls up to your new home,
so you can move inside!

Here's what you need

- Half-gallon (1.89 l) milk carton
- Pint (473 ml) milk carton
- Sticky-back Velcro®
- 2 paper fasteners
- Rubber band
- 3 sets wheels (page 17 or 18)
- Scissors

Many moving vans have padding on the walls so furniture won't be scratched during the trip. Some moving vans are so large they can move a car along with furniture, dishes, and other family belongings.

Here's what you do

1 Rinse, dry, and open spouts on milk cartons. Make a cab from the pint carton (page 16). Attach 1 set of wheels.

2 Cut away 2 opposite spout flaps from the half-gallon carton. Attach 2 sets of wheels to half-gallon carton.

❸ Attach fasteners to spout flaps and then wrap a rubber band around to hold flaps closed. Attach cab to half-gallon carton with sticky-back Velcro®.

NOW TRY THIS

❍ If someone moves into your neighborhood or into your classroom, invite him or her to play with you and your friends. There's always room for a new friend.

❍ Fill your milk carton van with photos and small mementos. Then deliver it to a friend who is moving away.

❍ If you were moving, what family belonging would be your most precious treasure? What would be the smallest thing to move? What would be the largest?

Pickup Truck

When you see a pickup truck
traveling on the road,
Passengers ride up in front,
while the rear holds the load!

Here's what you need

- Half-pint (236 ml) milk carton
- Pasta box
- Egg carton lid
- Sticky-back Velcro®
- 3 sets wheels (page 17 or 18)
- Tape
- Scissors

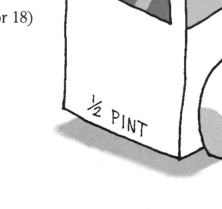

½ PINT

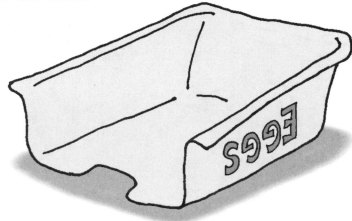

❷ Cut the pasta box and egg carton lid in half horizontally.

Here's what you do

❶ Rinse, dry, and open spouts on milk carton. Make a cab from the half-pint carton (page 16). Attach 1 set of wheels.

PASTA

❸ Tape egg carton lid onto pasta box. Attach 2 sets of wheels. Attach cab to pasta box with Velcro®.

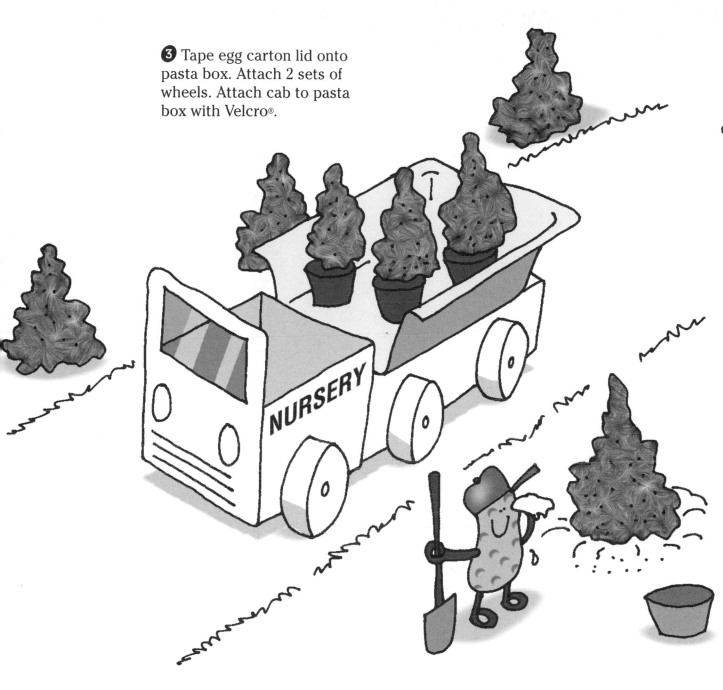

◐ Fill your pickup truck with things such as pebbles, Popsicle sticks, acorns, or sea shells. Or, fill it with treats like raisins or chocolate chips and make a delivery – to your room!

◐ Make a pickup truck from 2 boxes large enough to sit inside. Cut away the flaps from 1 box for a cab. Cut a second box in half horizontally and tape it to the cab. Tape large paper plates on the sides of the boxes for wheels. Fill up 1 box and sit in the other.

◐ Look in a pickup truck and you can tell a lot about a person. Play "Pickup Truck" with a friend. One person says what is in the truck; the other guesses what the person likes to do.

Tractor-Trailer Truck

Big rigs have full trailers
when they hit the road,
Then they drive cross-country
to drop off their load!

Here's what you need

- Half-gallon (1.89 l) milk carton
- Quart (946 ml) milk carton
- Pasta box
- Straw
- 5 sets wheels (page 17 or 18)
- Tape
- Sticky-back Velcro®
- Scissors

Here's what you do

❶ Rinse, dry, and open spouts on milk cartons. Cut away 2 opposite spout flaps from quart carton. Cut pasta box the length of the quart carton.

IN THE BEGINNING

Long before tractor-trailer trucks were crisscrossing North America, big, heavy loads of everything from oranges to coal were transported by train.

2 To make cab, cut away 3 flaps from half-gallon carton. Then cut halfway into carton along both sides of remaining flap.

3 Bend flap down and tape to hold; then follow curve and cut away carton's corners. Cut windows in sides of cab. Attach 2 sets of wheels.

HALF GALLON

CONTINUED ➡

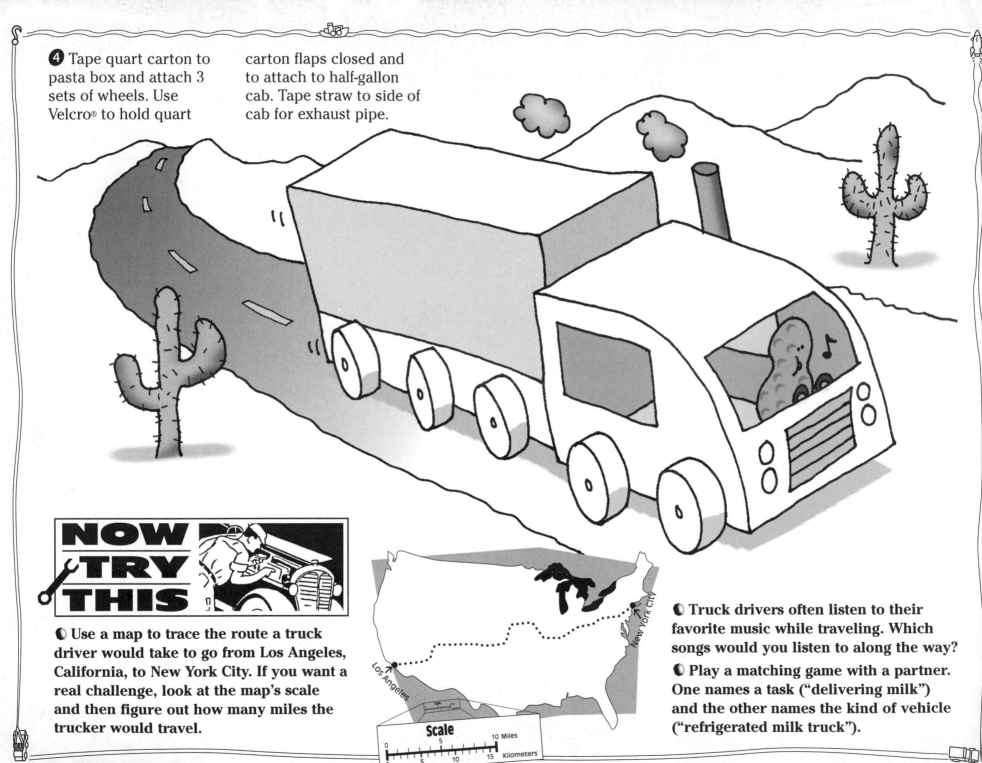

4 Tape quart carton to pasta box and attach 3 sets of wheels. Use Velcro® to hold quart carton flaps closed and to attach to half-gallon cab. Tape straw to side of cab for exhaust pipe.

NOW TRY THIS

🔴 Use a map to trace the route a truck driver would take to go from Los Angeles, California, to New York City. If you want a real challenge, look at the map's scale and then figure out how many miles the trucker would travel.

🔴 Truck drivers often listen to their favorite music while traveling. Which songs would you listen to along the way?

🔴 Play a matching game with a partner. One names a task ("delivering milk") and the other names the kind of vehicle ("refrigerated milk truck").

New York City

Los Angeles

Scale

0   5   10 Miles

0   5   10   15 Kilometers

In The Water

Vroom! Vroom!

Set sail for far off places
across an ocean wide.
Adventures will await you
upon the other side.

Sailboat

Sailors navigate with stars
to show them where they are,
If the winds are very calm,
their boats don't go too far!

Here's what you need

- 2 half-gallon (1.89 l) milk cartons
- Straw
- Construction paper scrap
- Tape
- Scissors
- Nail or pointed tool

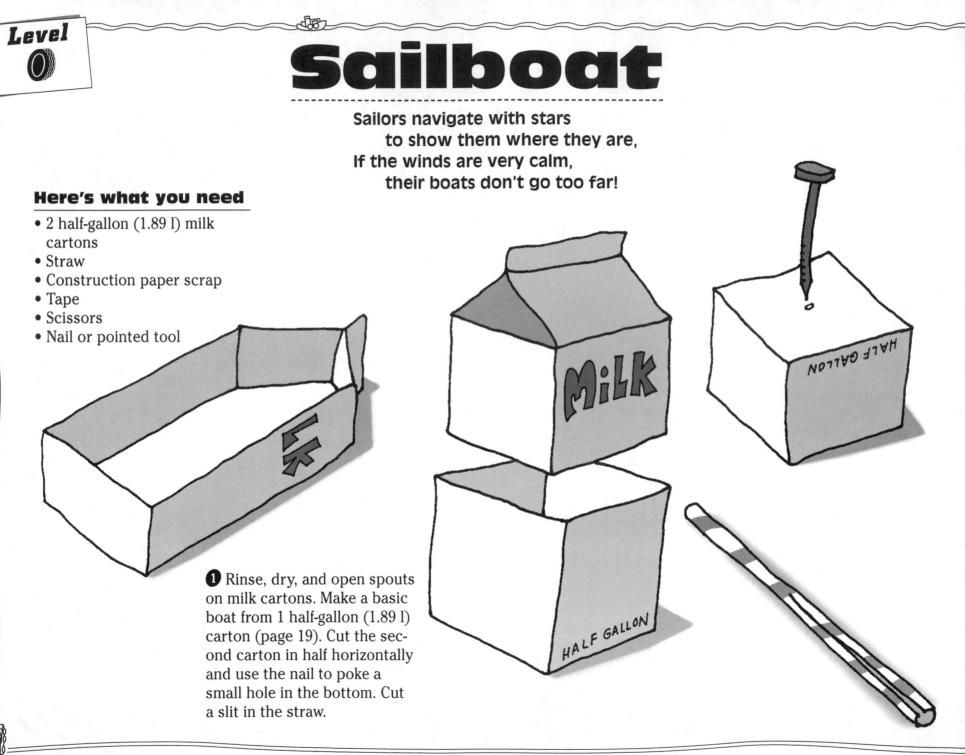

1 Rinse, dry, and open spouts on milk cartons. Make a basic boat from 1 half-gallon (1.89 l) carton (page 19). Cut the second carton in half horizontally and use the nail to poke a small hole in the bottom. Cut a slit in the straw.

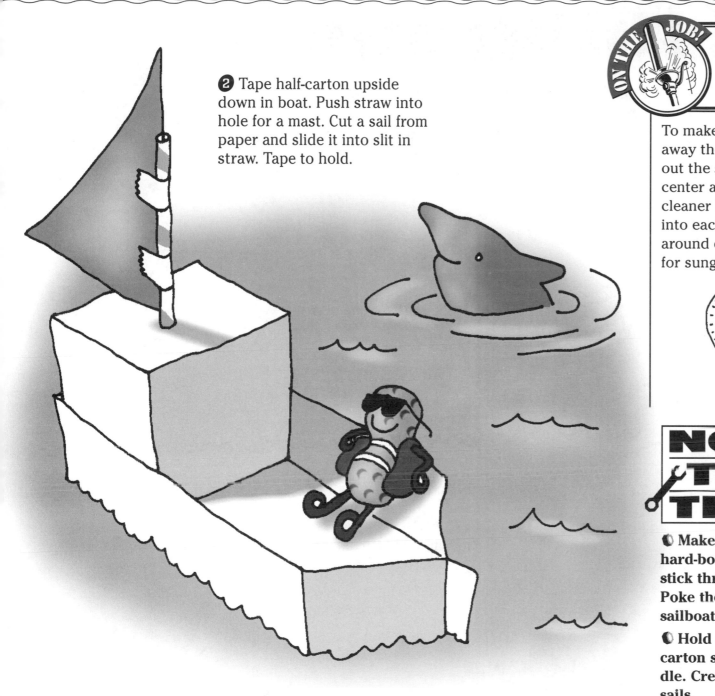

2 Tape half-carton upside down in boat. Push straw into hole for a mast. Cut a sail from paper and slide it into slit in straw. Tape to hold.

Sailor's sunglasses

To make some wearable sunglasses, cut away the rim of a heavy paper plate. Cut out the shape of glasses from the plate's center and cut out "glass;" cut the pipe cleaner in half. Poke a pipe cleaner half into each side of the glasses and bend to fit around ears. Glue on colored plastic wrap for sunglasses.

NOW TRY THIS

◐ Make delicious Egg Boats: Cut a hard-boiled egg in half. Put a thin pretzel stick through a slice of cheese for a sail. Poke the pretzel into the egg for a tasty sailboat treat.

◐ Hold a sailboat race. Make several milk carton sailboats and race them in a puddle. Create wind by blowing on the paper sails.

Fishing Boat

The fishermen will cast their nets
in ocean, lake, or bay,
The fish they catch are cleaned and sold
for dinner that same day!

Here's what you need

- 2 half-gallon (1.89 l) milk cartons
- Half-pint (236 ml) milk carton
- Nylon net or cheesecloth
- 2 straws
- Tape
- Scissors
- Nail or pointed tool
- Gummy fish candy (optional)

Here's what you do

❶ Rinse, dry, and open spouts on milk cartons. Make the basic boat from 1 half-gallon carton (page 19).

❷ Cut second half-gallon carton in half horizontally. Cut away spout flaps from half-pint carton. Use the nail to poke a hole in the bottom of both of these cartons.

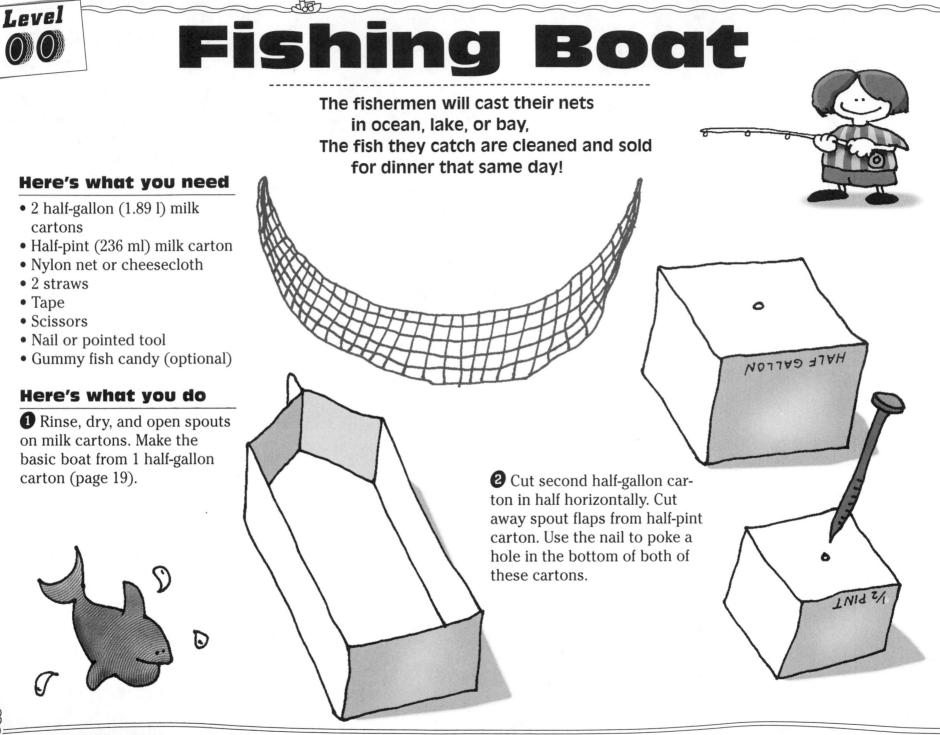

HALF GALLON

½ PINT

3 Tape cartons upside down in boat. Push straws through holes for masts. Tape nylon net between straws and add fish.

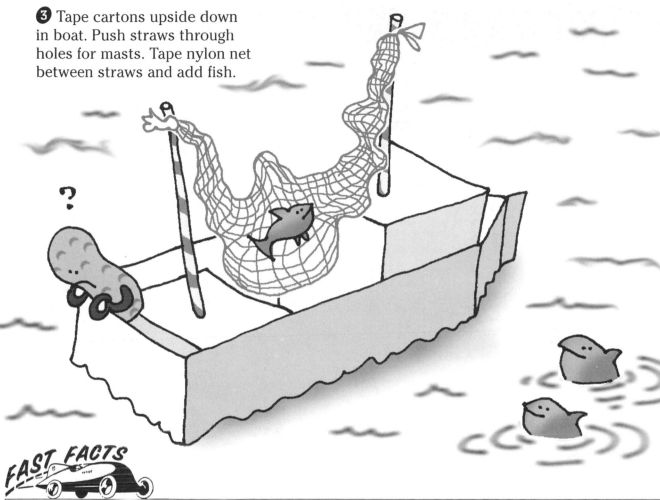

NOW TRY THIS

◐ Cut out fish shapes from construction paper and put a paper clip on each one. Next, attach 1 end of a string to a magnet and the other end to a stick for a fishing rod. Now, go fishing!

◐ Visit a pet store. Look at freshwater fish and saltwater fish. What are the differences that you notice?

◐ A "fish story" is usually told with great exaggeration ("I once caught a 30-pound (13.3 kg) fish," or "I used to walk 10 miles (16 kilometers) to school"). Listen to people talk and when something sounds exaggerated, ask if it is "a fish story."

FAST FACTS

Fishing boats are among the smallest boats that sail the sea. The "drifter" catches fish as they swim into long drift nets that hang in the water. The "trawler" uses a net that is dragged behind the boat as it moves through the water.

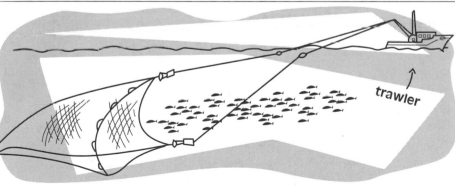

trawler

Barge

Barges travel slowly,
all they do is float,
Carrying a heavy load,
pushed by a tugboat!

Here's what you need

- Half-gallon (1.89 l) or quart (946 ml) milk carton
- String
- Nail or pointed tool
- Scissors

Here's what you do

❶ Rinse, dry, and open spout on milk carton. Make the basic boat (page 19).

❷ Use the nail to poke a hole through the carton spout. Tie a string through the hole to pull the barge.

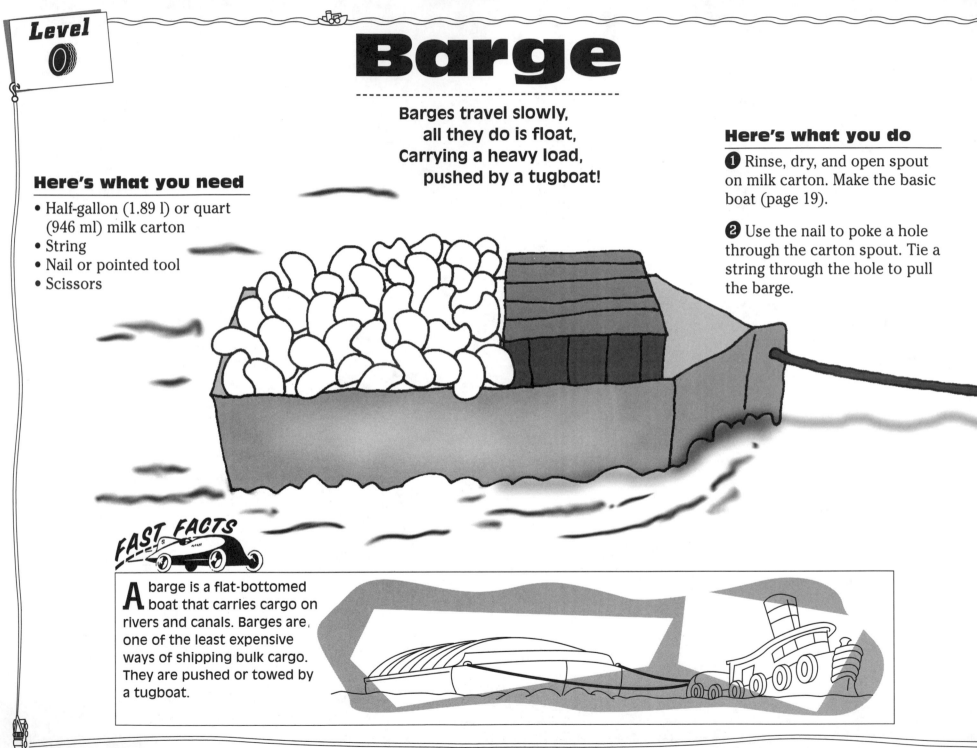

FAST FACTS

A barge is a flat-bottomed boat that carries cargo on rivers and canals. Barges are one of the least expensive ways of shipping bulk cargo. They are pushed or towed by a tugboat.

NOW TRY THIS

◐ **Load your milk carton barge with small objects and tow in a puddle.**

◐ **Become a tugboat: Push a cardboard box filled with pillows. Then, remove the pillows and fill with books. Do you use more energy with the heavier load?**

◐ **Read *Snowy* by Berlie Doherty to learn about adventures on a barge.**

Rowboat

Sit inside a rowboat
and use the oars to row,
You won't need a motor
to get this boat to go!

Here's what you need

- Pint (473 ml) milk carton
- 2 Popsicle sticks
- Tape
- Scissors
- Nail or pointed tool

Here's what you do

❶ Rinse, dry, and open spout on milk carton. Make the basic boat (page 19). Cut 1" (2.5 cm) off bottom of remaining half-carton for a bench. With nail, punch a small hole in each side of the boat.

FAST FACTS

A rowboat is a sturdy boat rowed with oars. The small rowboat that is often towed behind a sailboat or cruiser to get to shore is called a "dinghy."

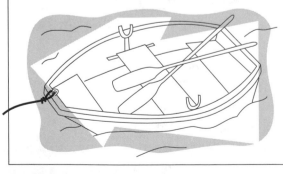

MILK

ONE PINT

2 Put Popsicle sticks through holes for oars. Tape bench inside boat.

◐ The oars of a rowboat steer the boat. Next time you are in the tub, float a toy boat. "Paddle" gently with your hand on the right side of the boat and notice which way the boat turns. Now try paddling on the left side.

◐ Teach a younger child "Row, Row, Row Your Boat." Then, try singing in a "round" with some friends.

Submarine

Travel in a submarine
and watch the fish swim by,
Come explore the ocean floor
while staying warm and dry!

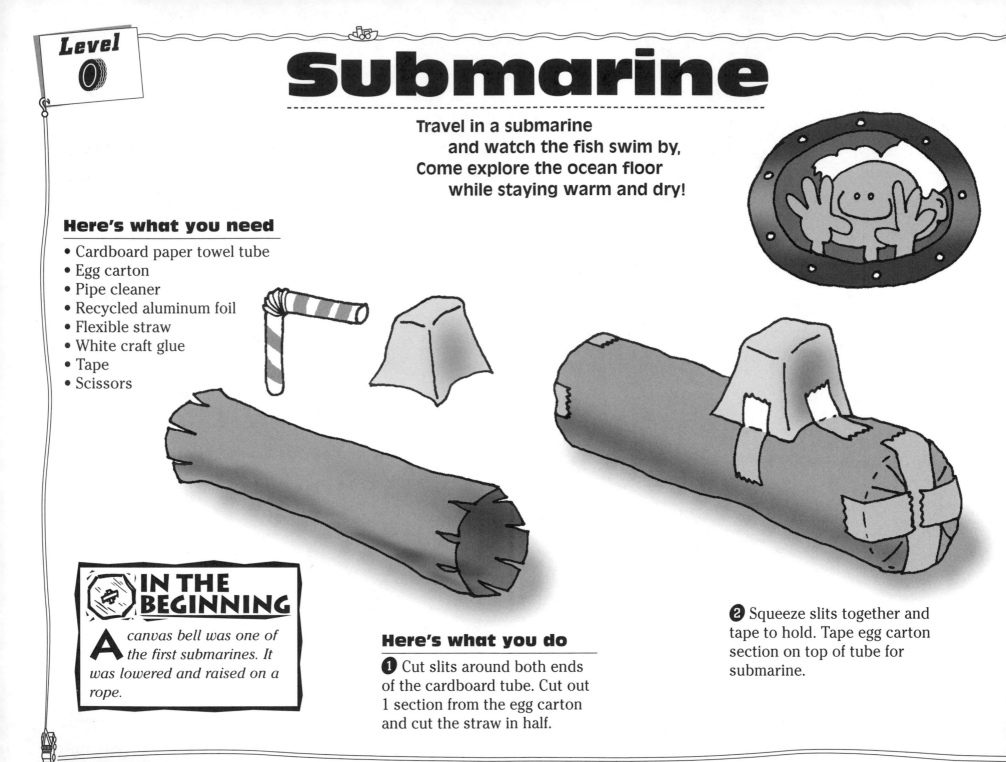

Here's what you need

- Cardboard paper towel tube
- Egg carton
- Pipe cleaner
- Recycled aluminum foil
- Flexible straw
- White craft glue
- Tape
- Scissors

IN THE BEGINNING

A canvas bell was one of the first submarines. It was lowered and raised on a rope.

Here's what you do

❶ Cut slits around both ends of the cardboard tube. Cut out 1 section from the egg carton and cut the straw in half.

❷ Squeeze slits together and tape to hold. Tape egg carton section on top of tube for submarine.

3 Wrap submarine in foil. Twist pipe cleaner and put in end of tube for a propeller. Put straw in top of submarine for a periscope.

NOW TRY THIS

◐ Make an underwater viewer: Cut out the bottom of a tall, plastic deli container. Cover 1 end with plastic wrap held in place with a rubber band. Use the container to look underwater in your bathtub or sink.

◐ For an underwater treat, make flavored gelatin in a clear bowl. Chill until it's almost firm. Push in foods such as gummy fish, grapes, mini-marshmallows, or blueberries.

◐ Cut out the center of 1 paper plate. Draw fish and plant life on a second plate. Tape plastic wrap on top of your drawing. Tape the first plate upside-down over the second plate for an undersea view through a porthole.

Tugboat

A little tugboat works so hard
it hasn't time to play,
It's busy pushing big barges
and docking boats all day!

Here's what you need

- 2 half-gallon (1.89 l) milk cartons
- Quart (946 ml) milk carton
- Cardboard paper towel tube
- Cotton ball
- Tape
- Scissors

Here's what you do

❶ Rinse, dry, and open spout on milk cartons. Make the basic boat from 1 half-gallon carton (page 19). Cut away two-thirds of the second half-gallon carton.

Milk

HALF GALLON

Milk

1 QUART

❷ Cut away two-thirds of the quart carton and, in the bottom, cut a hole the size of the cardboard tube.

Big ships are too clumsy to maneuver in the tight spaces alongside piers. The smaller tugboats guide them, often pushing with their padded bows against the ship. Or, they are used to pull a whole string of barges.

NOW TRY THIS

◐ Float a few milk carton barges (page 82) and see how many of them the tugboat can push at one time.

◐ Here's a way to get a feeling for the difficulty a tugboat crew faces when it docks a large ship in a busy harbor: Lay out an obstacle course with chairs. Using only your feet, move a cardboard carton across the room.

3 Tape cartons upside-down in the boat. Push the cardboard tube through the hole for a smokestack. Put cotton ball in top of tube for smoke.

TUGS·R·US

Cruise Liner

Go aboard a cruise liner
for travel and some fun,
You will meet many new friends,
and have fun in the sun!

Here's what you need

- Half-gallon (1.89 l) milk carton
- Cardboard pasta box
- Recycled aluminum foil
- Cardboard toilet tissue tube
- White craft glue
- Paper scraps
- Cotton balls
- Tape
- Scissors

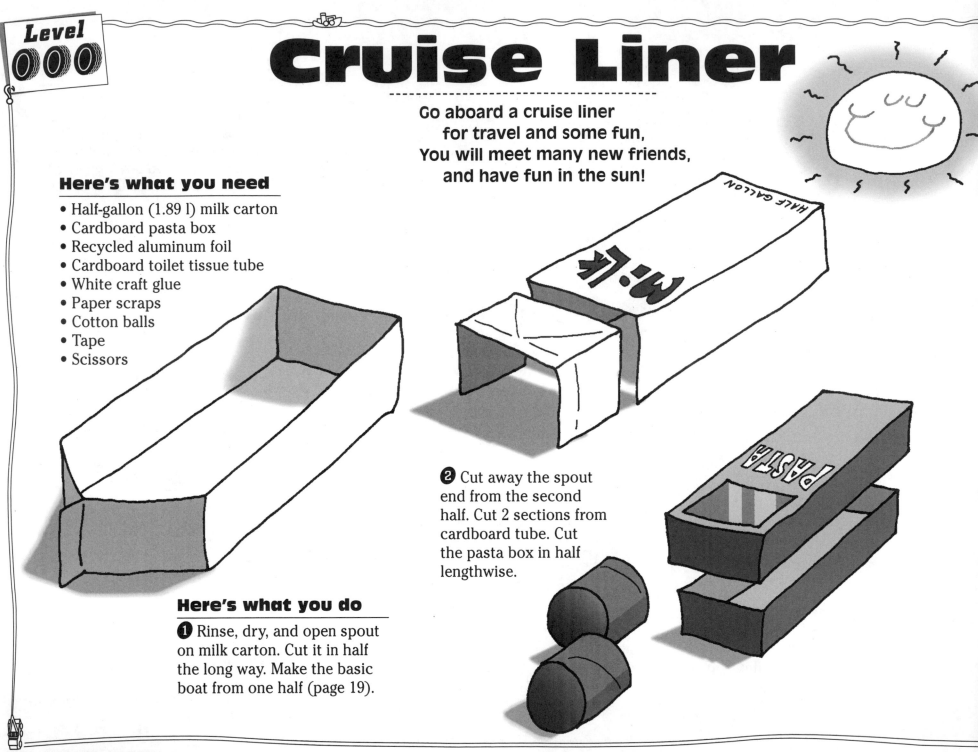

❷ Cut away the spout end from the second half. Cut 2 sections from cardboard tube. Cut the pasta box in half lengthwise.

Here's what you do

❶ Rinse, dry, and open spout on milk carton. Cut it in half the long way. Make the basic boat from one half (page 19).

3 Put half-carton upside-down inside boat. Tape pasta box on top. Wrap boat in foil.

CONTINUED ▶

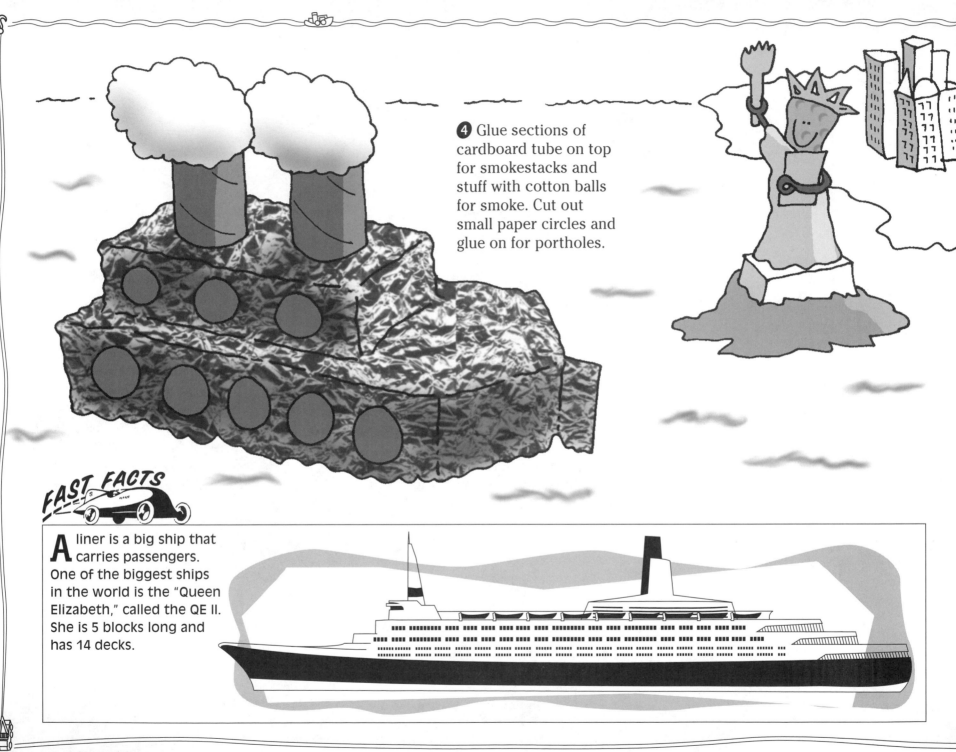

4 Glue sections of cardboard tube on top for smokestacks and stuff with cotton balls for smoke. Cut out small paper circles and glue on for portholes.

FAST FACTS

A liner is a big ship that carries passengers. One of the biggest ships in the world is the "Queen Elizabeth," called the QE II. She is 5 blocks long and has 14 decks.

NOW TRY THIS

◐ Make your cruise liner with many decks on top and add some passengers.

◐ Paint a picture of a blue sky, an ocean harbor, and a beach. Draw or cut out pictures of different kinds of boats for your painting.

◐ Start a collection of postcards from far-off places. Ask your friends and family to save them for you. Sort them into groups such as beaches, animals, buildings.

Raft

Rafts float on the water
and drift away from shore,
If you head the wrong way,
just paddle with an oar.

Here's what you need

- Egg carton lid
- Popsicle sticks
- White craft glue
- Restaurant stir stick
- Construction paper scraps
- Tape
- Paper fastener
- Yarn
- Scissors

Here's what you do

❶ Cut the egg carton lid in half, leaving center hump attached. Using the half with the hump, cut down sides, leaving a short edge all around. Cut out a construction paper sail.

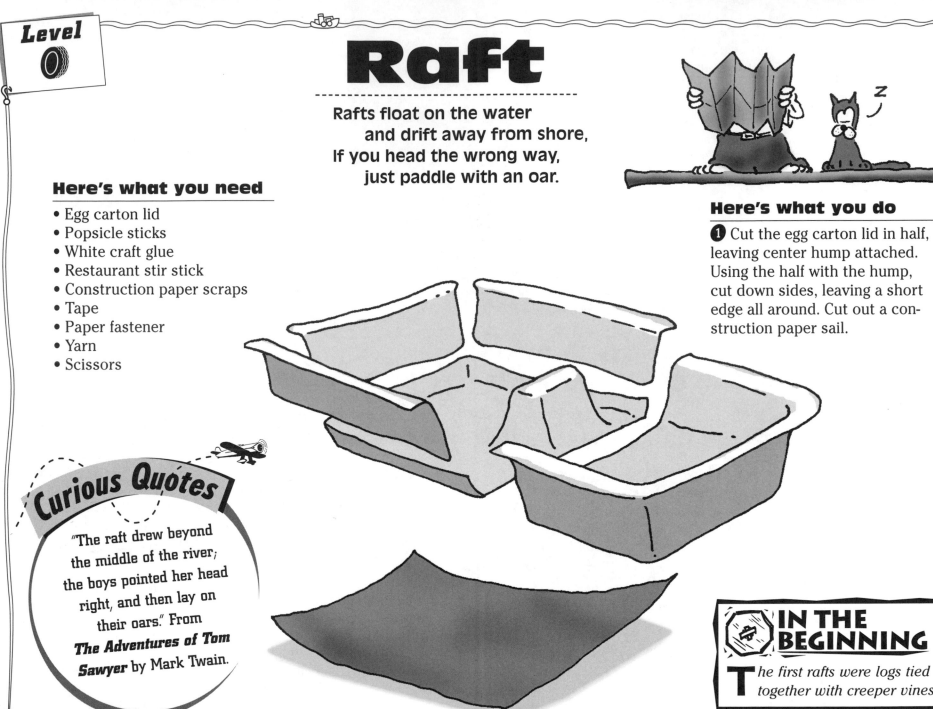

Curious Quotes

"The raft drew beyond the middle of the river; the boys pointed her head right, and then lay on their oars." From *The Adventures of Tom Sawyer* by Mark Twain.

IN THE BEGINNING

The first rafts were logs tied together with creeper vines.

2 Glue Popsicle sticks onto cut-down lid. Poke stir stick into raft and tape on sail. Allow to dry completely.

3 Attach yarn with paper fastener to pull raft.

NOW TRY THIS

● No matter how old you are, you are never too old to have a great book read to you. Ask a grown-up to read you a chapter at a time from Mark Twain's *The Adventures of Tom Sawyer* or *The Adventures of Huck Finn*. You won't believe the mischief they get into!

● Take turns telling about your dream adventure, if you could do whatever you wanted.

● Make the raft, only this time gather small twigs to use instead of Popsicle sticks.

Viking Ship

Viking ships sailed the seas
many years ago,
Vikings wore their helmets,
and used oars to row!

Here's what you need

- Half-gallon (1.89 l) milk carton
- Cardboard toilet tissue tube
- Drinking straw
- Construction paper scrap
- Tape
- Popsicle sticks
- Scissors

Here's what you do

❶ Rinse, dry, and open spout on milk carton. Make the basic boat (page 19).

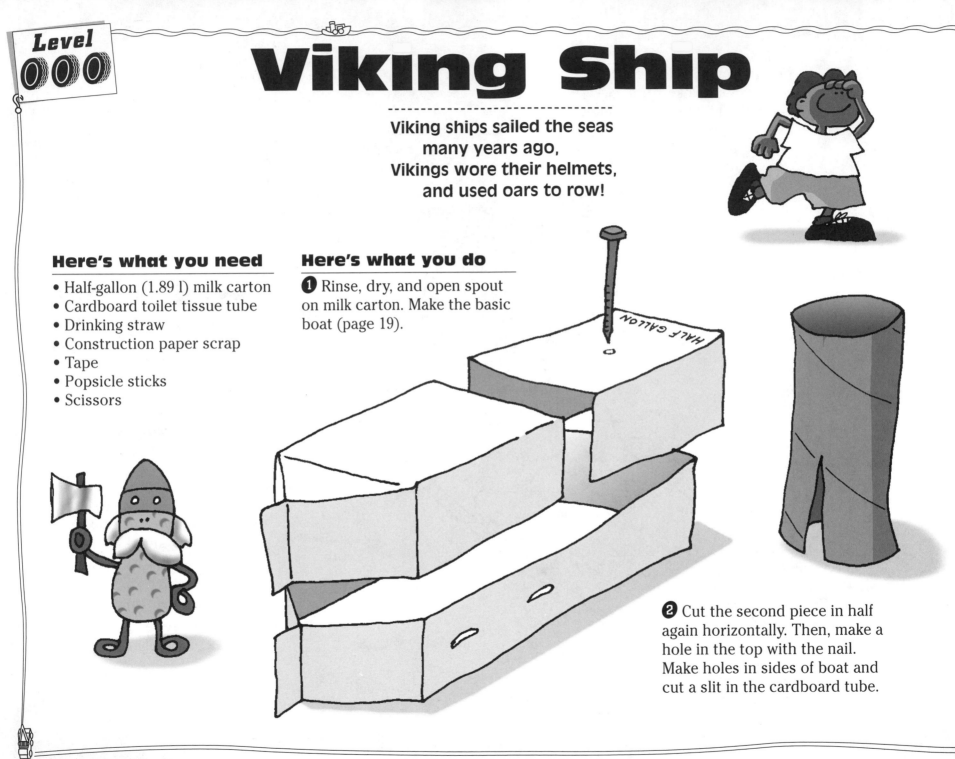

HALF GALLON

❷ Cut the second piece in half again horizontally. Then, make a hole in the top with the nail. Make holes in sides of boat and cut a slit in the cardboard tube.

3 Put quarter piece upside-down in boat and push straw through hole. Make construction paper sail and attach to the straw. Put Popsicle sticks in holes for oars.

CONTINUED ▷

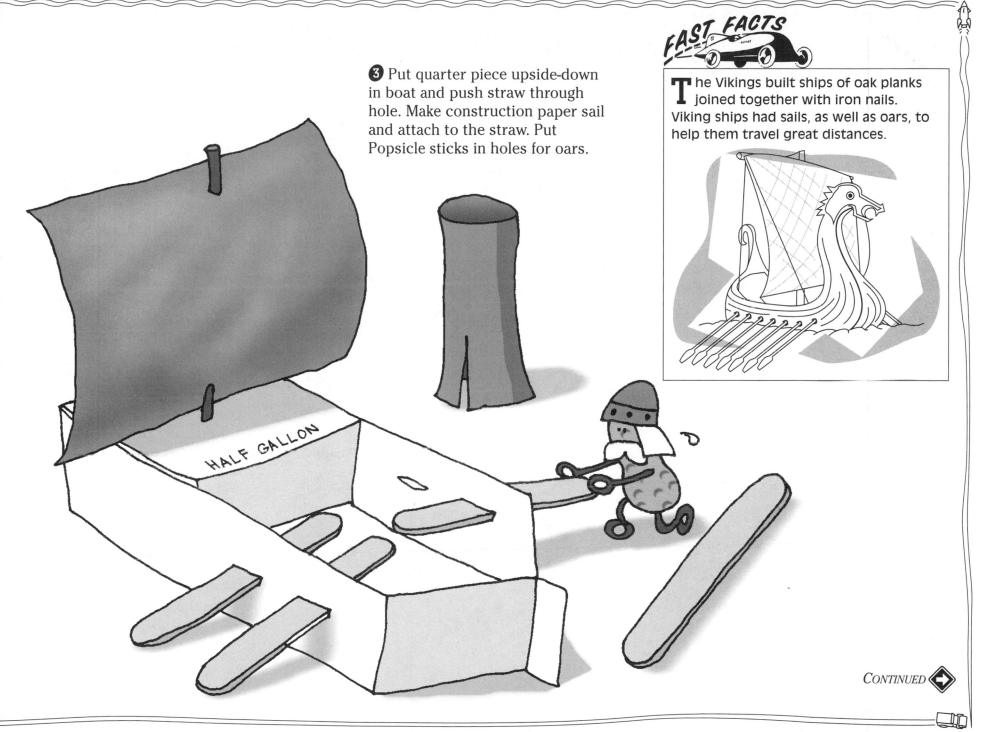

The Vikings built ships of oak planks joined together with iron nails. Viking ships had sails, as well as oars, to help them travel great distances.

HALF GALLON

④ Decorate cardboard roll as figurehead (see "NOW TRY THIS"). Slide onto bow of boat and tape to hold.

NOW TRY THIS

◑ The prow, or front end, of a Viking warship curved gracefully upward and ended with a wood carving, or figurehead, of the head of a dragon or snake. Use markers to design an unusual creature you can put on the front of your boat.

◑ Cut a Viking's shield from cardboard. Tape a strip of cardboard to the back for a hand grip and wrap your shield in recycled foil.

◑ Vikings set sail from Scandinavian countries. To make Norwegian cookies called "Kringla," prepare a butter cookie batter. Then, twist the dough in the shape of a pretzel and bake.

Vroom!
Vroom!

Through The Air

Birds and bees and butterflies
are flying through the air.
Rockets, planes, hot-air balloons
are also way up there!

Flying Saucer

If a flying saucer lands
and spacemen are inside,
Welcome them and say, "Hello,
let's all go for a ride!"

Here's what you need

- 2 heavy paper plates
- Paper bowl
- Tape or stapler
- Scissors
- Tinted plastic wrap (optional)

IN THE BEGINNING

On the night of November 17, 1896, a group of men were driving a team of horses across the open plains near Sacramento, California. They reported seeing bright lights and a strange object in the sky and hearing humans' singing. This was one of the first reported sightings of a U.F.O.

Here's what you do

❶ Cut out openings around sides and top of paper bowl for windows. Cover windows with plastic wrap.

Flying saucers are also known as U.F.O.'s (unidentified flying objects). Some people believe they may be spaceships from other planets.

NOW TRY THIS

◐ **Make several flying saucers and test them to see which one can fly the farthest.**

◐ **Spread cream cheese on pita bread. Use olives, slices of red or green peppers, celery, and carrot sticks to make a tasty "flying saucer" sandwich.**

◐ **Use poster paint to paint a "man-in-the-moon" face on a smooth, flat rock.**

❷ Tape or staple 1 plate upside-down on top of second plate. Then tape bowl on top of plates.

Jet Plane

Taxi down the runway,
    then lift up off the ground.
Big engines screech and roar,
    jets break the speed of sound!

Here's what you need

- Styrofoam plate
- Recycled aluminum foil
- Tape
- Scissors
- Pencil

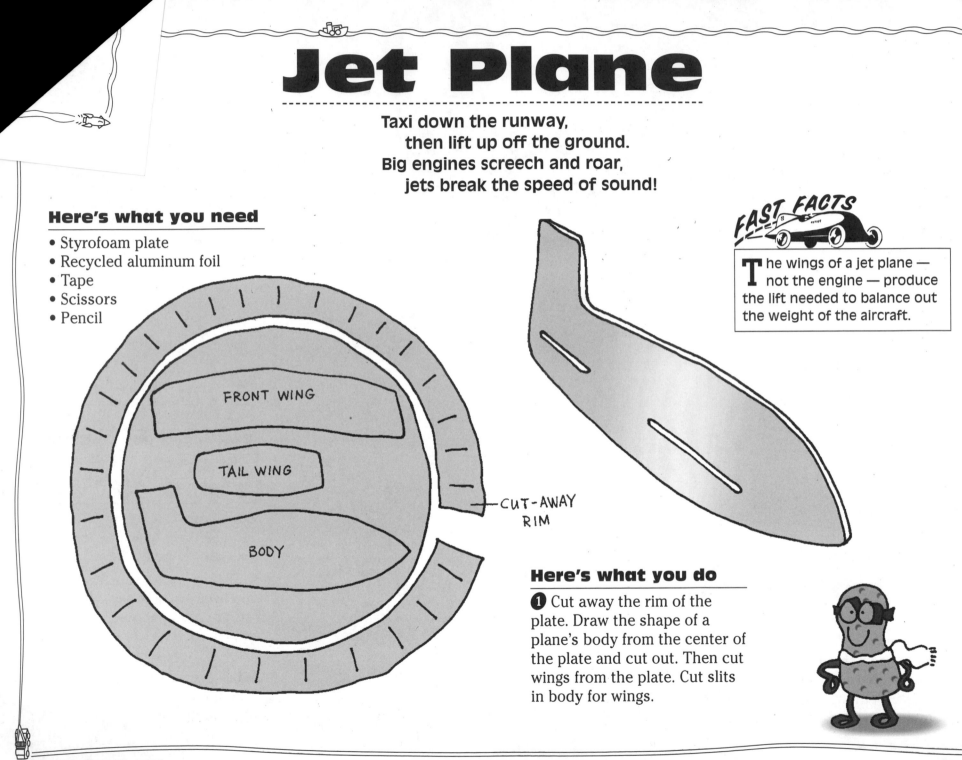

FRONT WING

TAIL WING

CUT-AWAY RIM

BODY

FAST FACTS

The wings of a jet plane — not the engine — produce the lift needed to balance out the weight of the aircraft.

Here's what you do

❶ Cut away the rim of the plate. Draw the shape of a plane's body from the center of the plate and cut out. Then cut wings from the plate. Cut slits in body for wings.

2 Wrap wings and body of plane in foil and tape to hold. Slide wings through slits in plane.

NOW TRY THIS

◐ Fly your plane from a hilltop outdoors or while standing on a chair.

◐ To get an idea of how an airplane wing works, blow hard just above a sheet of paper. Your breath is like the fast air above a wing. There is less air on top, so the paper is lifted up by the air below.

Space Shuttle

Shuttles on the launch pad
blast off through the sky,
Astronauts strapped inside
smile and wave goodbye!

Here's what you need

- Cardboard toilet tissue tube
- Shirt cardboard scrap
- Recycled aluminum foil
- Tissue paper streamers
  (red, orange, yellow)
- Tape
- Scissors

Here's what you do

❶ Cut slits around 1 end of the tube and then cut a slit in other end at top. From shirt cardboard, cut out the shuttle's wings the same length as the cardboard tube and cut out a triangle, too.

NOW TRY THIS

◐ Fill a small bag with dried fruits, nuts, and raisins for a "freeze-dried" space food snack.

◐ If you are interested in becoming an astronaut, read the biographies of John Glenn, Neil Armstrong, or Sally Ride.

FAST FACTS

The space shuttle, a combination rocket ship and aircraft, is launched from Earth by rockets and then travels to an orbiting point beyond the influence of Earth's gravity.

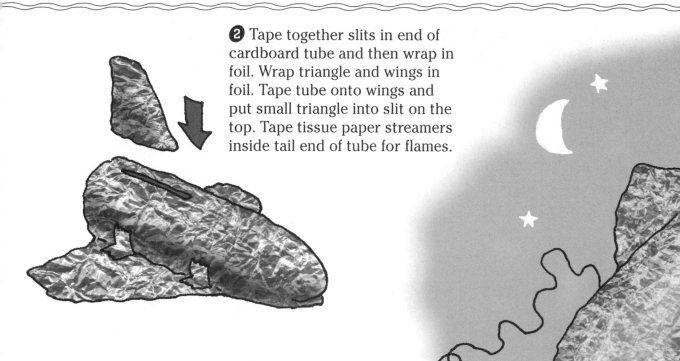

❷ Tape together slits in end of cardboard tube and then wrap in foil. Wrap triangle and wings in foil. Tape tube onto wings and put small triangle into slit on the top. Tape tissue paper streamers inside tail end of tube for flames.

Space helmet

To make a space helmet that you can wear, cut out the front, back, and side panels from a cereal box. Cut front and back panels in half vertically and cut side panels in half horizontally.

Tape 4 front and back pieces

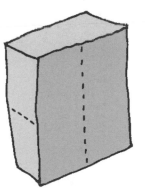

together to form a cross shape. Tape each side panel between ends of cross for a helmet. Then, cut out an opening between 2 panels for the face. Wrap helmet in foil, tape to hold, and blast off!

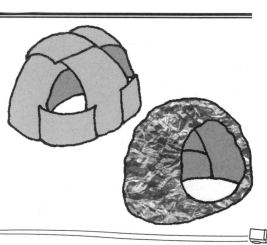

Helicopter

Helicopters are whirlybirds,
their blades spin round and round,
They fly much lower than a jet,
and lift straight off the ground!

Here's what you need

- Pint (473 ml) milk carton
- Toothpaste box
- Shirt cardboard scrap
- Recycled aluminum foil
- 2 drinking straws
- Paper fastener
- Pipe cleaner
- 2 Popsicle sticks
- Scissors

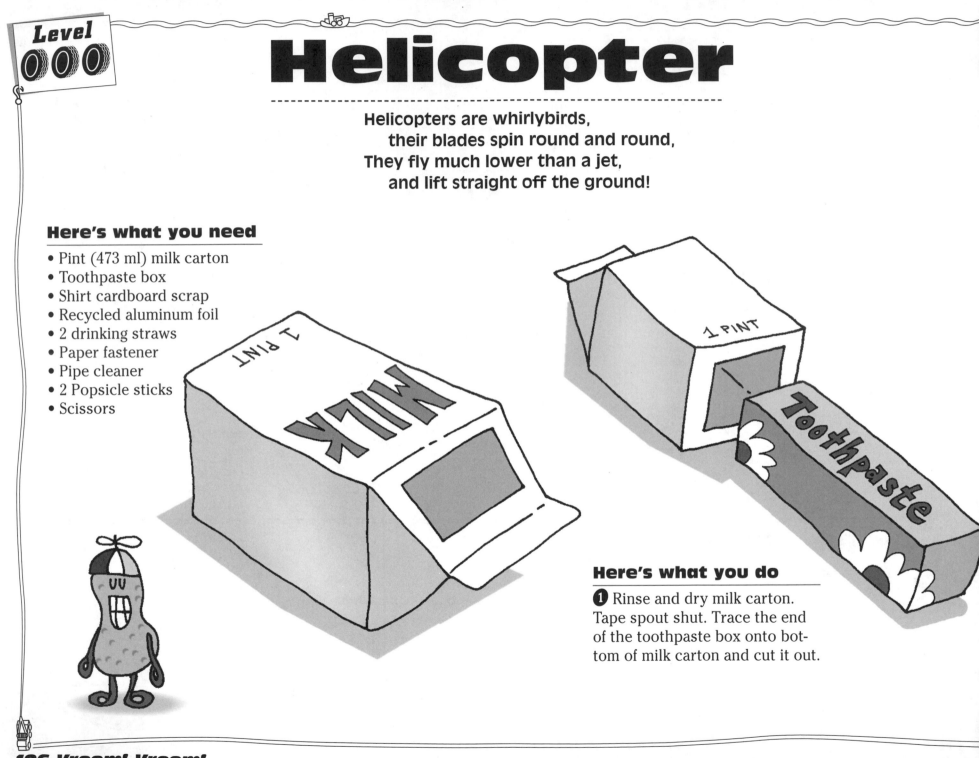

Here's what you do

❶ Rinse and dry milk carton. Tape spout shut. Trace the end of the toothpaste box onto bottom of milk carton and cut it out.

2 Cut the straw in half. Cut 2 sets of blades from cardboard.

CONTINUED ➡

IN THE BEGINNING

Over 500 years ago, in 1483, Leonardo da Vinci, an Italian artist and inventor, made a drawing of a very simple helicopter. The first helicopter to get off the ground was made in 1907 by two Frenchmen.

3 Wrap blades in foil. Attach 1 set to side of toothpaste box with paper fastener, and attach second set to pipe cleaner.

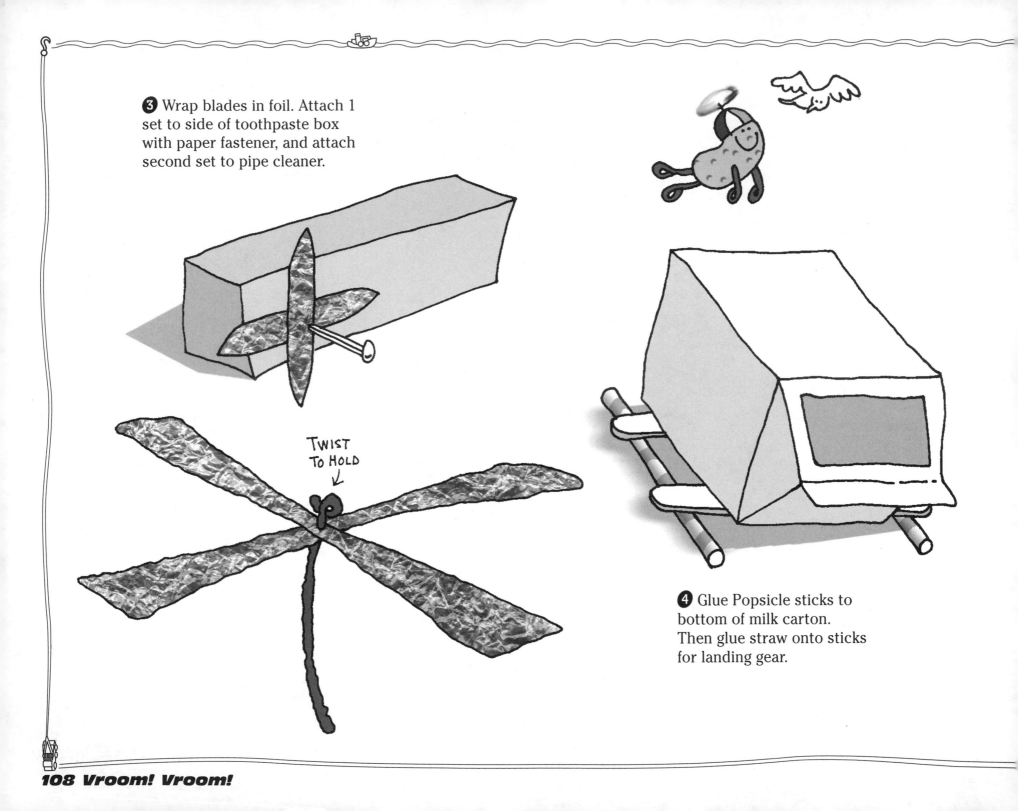

TWIST TO HOLD

4 Glue Popsicle sticks to bottom of milk carton. Then glue straw onto sticks for landing gear.

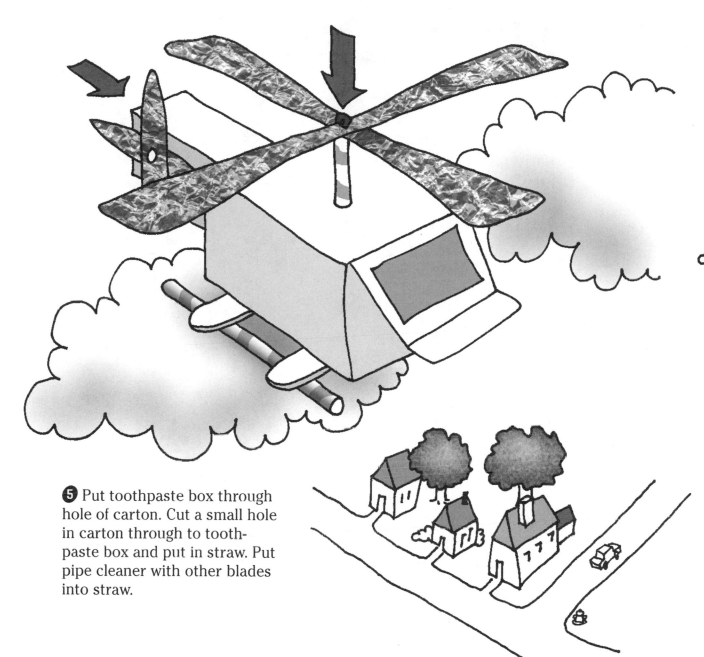

5 Put toothpaste box through hole of carton. Cut a small hole in carton through to toothpaste box and put in straw. Put pipe cleaner with other blades into straw.

NOW TRY THIS

❶ In autumn you can find seed pods from maple trees that spin to the ground like a helicopter.

❷ Cut a piece of paper in the shape of a T with a small V-cut in the top. Attach a paper clip to the bottom of the T. Toss the paper helicopter up in the air and watch it spin to the ground.

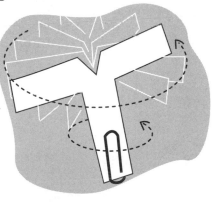

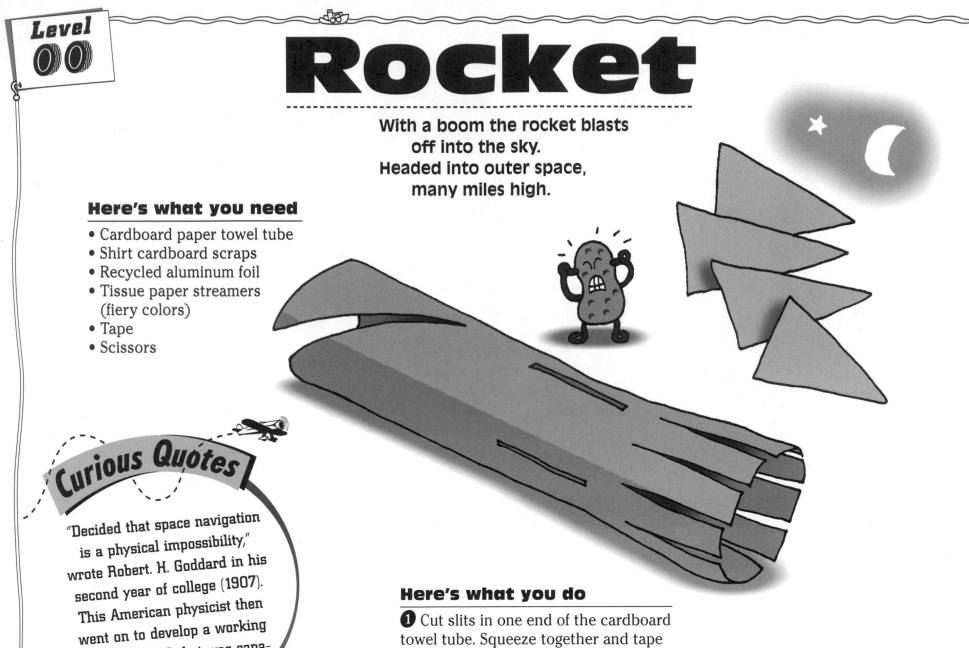

Rocket

With a boom the rocket blasts
off into the sky.
Headed into outer space,
many miles high.

Here's what you need

- Cardboard paper towel tube
- Shirt cardboard scraps
- Recycled aluminum foil
- Tissue paper streamers
  (fiery colors)
- Tape
- Scissors

Curious Quotes

"Decided that space navigation is a physical impossibility," wrote Robert. H. Goddard in his second year of college (1907). This American physicist then went on to develop a working rocket in 1926 that was capable of reaching space.

Here's what you do

❶ Cut slits in one end of the cardboard towel tube. Squeeze together and tape to form nose. Cut 4 slits around the nose. Make 2 diagonal cuts on opposite sides of the other end of tube. Cut 4 cardboard triangles.

2 Cover towel tube and triangles in foil. Put triangles into slits around nose and bend back flaps at bottom of tube for rocket to stand upright. Tape tissue paper streamers inside tube for flame.

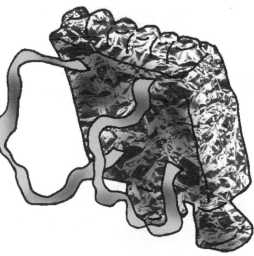

Jet pack

To make a jet pack, string ribbons through 4 holes cut in each corner of a cereal box. Tape ribbons inside box; tape lid closed. Cut 6 sections in a row from an egg carton and tape to top of cereal box. Tape 2 paper cups to box bottom. Wrap all in foil. Slide arms through ribbons to wear the jet pack.

NOW TRY THIS

◐ Have a rocket party. Everyone can make a rocket and then launch them together with paper confetti. Count together backwards from 10 to 1. At 1, shout, "Blast off!" and toss the confetti high in the air.

◐ For a special dessert that's "out of this world," cut a plain sheet cake in the shape of a rocket. Frost with your favorite icing and decorate with small candies and red licorice "flames."

Hot-Air Balloon

Ride in a hot-air balloon
and drift across the sky,
Safe inside the gondola
you'll float a mile high!

Here's what you need

- Construction paper
- Tissue paper
- 2 drinking straws
- 1 plastic dessert cup
- Tape
- White craft glue
- Scissors

Here's what you do

❶ Fold construction paper in half lengthwise. Cut slits 1" (2.5 cm) apart, beginning each slit at fold and stopping 1" (2.5 cm) from the edge of the paper.

IN THE BEGINNING

In 1978, three Americans made the first successful crossing of the Atlantic Ocean in a balloon named Double Eagle. The journey from the U.S.A. to France took six days.

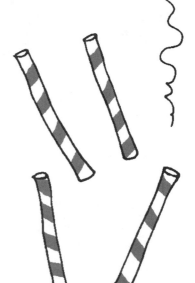

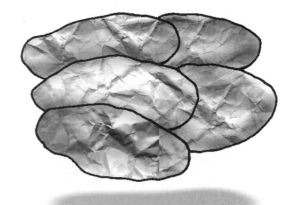

❷ Cut straws into 4 equal pieces and tissue paper into several oval shapes.

3 Open the construction paper and tape together vertically for a lantern shape.

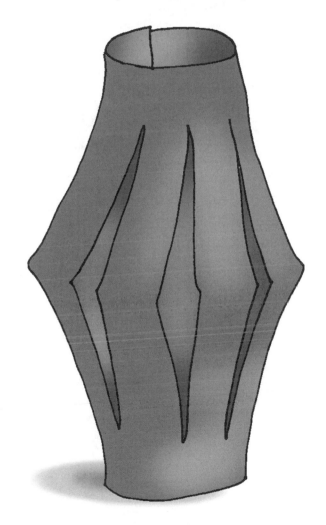

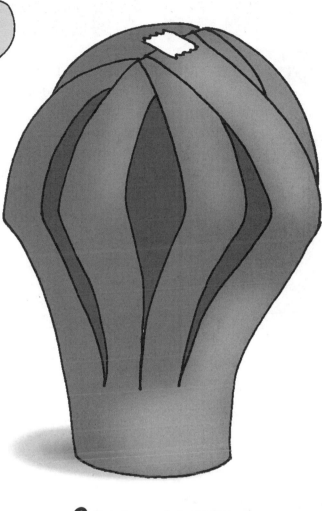

Because it is lighter than cold air, the hot air, warmed by a gas burner, causes the balloon to rise.

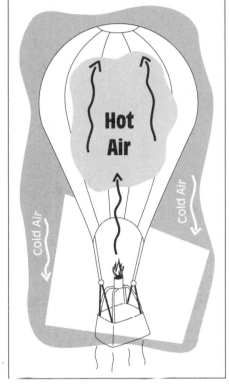

Hot Air

Cold Air

Cold Air

4 Cut through top slits of lantern and gather strips of paper together in center. Tape to hold for balloon.

CONTINUED ➧

5 Glue tissue paper ovals between construction paper strips. Tape straws inside dessert cup and to base of balloon for gondola.

NOW TRY THIS

◐ Decorate your hot-air balloon with shiny stars and colorful stickers.

◐ When you're high up in a balloon, things on the ground look very different. Draw a map of your street as if you were looking down from a hot-air balloon.

◐ For a larger gondola, use a plastic berry basket, paper cup, or a half-pint (236 ml) milk carton.

Just Plain Folks!

Vroom! Vroom!

Passengers sit in rear seats,
heads bob up and down.
Drivers sit up in the front,
taking folks through town.

Peanut Passengers

Peanuts make a great snack,
that's very good to eat.
When you draw on the shells
these passengers are neat!

Here's what you need

- Peanuts (in shell)
- Markers
- Pipe cleaner
- Scrap yarn
- White craft glue
- Scissors

Here's what you do

❶ Cut 4 short pieces of pipe cleaner. Dip ends into glue and poke into sides of shell for arms and legs.

❷ Use marker to draw a face on the shell. Glue on yarn for hair.

NOW TRY THIS

◖ Make a bunch of peanut passengers and put them in the school bus or double-decker bus (pages 22 and 28).

◖ Make a batch of peanut butter: Put 1 cup (250 ml) of shelled, raw, or roasted peanuts in a blender or food processor. Add a few drops of oil and a pinch of salt. Blend until it is the consistency you like.

Clothespin Farmer

Clothespins hold wash on the line
as windy breezes blow,
If you dress them up you'll see
a farmer that you know!

Here's what you need

- Wooden clothespin (non-spring)
- Pipe cleaner
- Peanut (in shell)
- Markers
- Construction paper scraps (blue, red, brown)
- White craft glue
- Restaurant stir stick
- Scissors

Here's what you do

❶ Wrap blue construction paper around legs of clothespin and tape to hold. Fold a rectangle of red paper in half; then cut out a T-shape with a small opening in top for a shirt.

❷ Put shirt on clothespin. Cut pipe cleaner and tape into sleeves for arms. Tape sides of shirt together.

❸ Cut a donut shape from brown paper for a hat brim. Glue half of a peanut shell on top.

❹ Tape a paper pitchfork to a stir stick and put in farmer's hand. Use markers to draw on farmer's face and hair.

NOW TRY THIS

◗ Use clothespins to create many different characters such as a cowboy, an astronaut, a doctor, or a dancer.

◗ Make a clothespin butterfly. Accordion-fold a sheet of paper towel. Dip the corners in food color and allow to dry. Glue the towel in the center of the clothespin; then spread open the butterfly's "wings."

Wooden Ice-Cream Spoon Fire Fighter

**Wooden ice-cream spoons are great
for getting every drop,
They can be used as people, too,
with faces drawn on top!**

Here's what you need

- Wooden ice-cream spoon
- Markers
- Construction paper scraps
  (red, black)
- Recycled aluminum foil scrap
- Pipe cleaner
- White craft glue
- Scissors

Here's what you do

❶ Cut a small oval from red construction paper for a hat. Cut a badge from foil.

❷ Cut a U-shape in the hat, bend paper forward, and glue foil badge on hat.

❸ Fold a rectangle of black paper in half and cut out a T-shape with a small opening in top for a fire fighter's slicker.

4 Cut pipe cleaners into 4 pieces and tape onto spoon for arms and legs.

5 Put slicker on spoon and tape sides together. Cut foil circles and glue onto slicker for buttons.

6 Glue fire fighter's hat onto spoon and use markers to draw on face.

Fire fighter's helmet

To make a wearable helmet, fold a 9" x 12" (22.5 cm x 30 cm) piece of construction paper in half vertically. Cut away corners opposite fold and then cut an oval shape into the folded edge. Cut a badge from foil. Lay paper flat, bend center flap upright, and glue on badge.

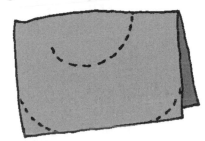

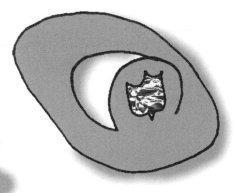

Pom-Pom Race Car Driver

Put together pom-poms
with a little dab of glue
To make a fuzzy driver
who's round and cuddly, too!

Here's what you need

- 1 plastic dessert cup
- Pom-poms (1 large, 1 small)
- Pipe cleaner
- Shirt cardboard scrap
- White craft glue
- Scissors
- Wiggly eyes (optional)

Here's what you do

1 Cut a small hole in both sides of the dessert cup. Turn the cup upside-down and put the pipe cleaner through holes for arms.

2 Glue the large pom-pom on top of the cup for a head. Glue on wiggly eyes and a small pom-pom for a nose. Cut out a cardboard steering wheel and wrap pipe cleaner arms around it.

NOW TRY THIS

❶ Make a menagerie of bugs and birds with different-colored and different-sized pom-poms.

❷ Use 3 paper cups and 1 pom-pom to play, "Hide The Pom-Pom." Turn the cups upside down, placing the pom-pom under 1 of the cups. Move the cups around and try to guess which cup the pom-pom is under.

FAST FACTS

A race car driver wears a fireproof suit with close-fitting gloves, light-weight boots, and a strong, lightweight crash helmet.

Cardboard Cutout Construction Worker

Construction workers start at dawn
and work hard every day,
They make the roads our cars ride on
and places where we play!

Here's what you need

- Shirt cardboard scrap
- 1 plastic dessert cup
- Pipe cleaner
- Markers
- Scissors

Here's what you do

1 From cardboard, cut out a steering wheel and the profile (side view) of a construction worker wearing a hard hat. Cut a slit across the top of the dessert cup.

2 Put a pipe cleaner through a hole cut in the center of the cardboard construction worker for arms. Wrap arms around cardboard steering wheel. Stand construction worker in slit in cup.

FAST FACTS

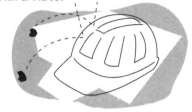

Workers operating big machinery usually wear special protective clothing such as heavy gloves, steel-toed boots, thick pants, shirts with long sleeves, and hard hats.

NOW TRY THIS

❂ To make building blocks, cut away the top of 2 milk cartons that are the same size. Slide one carton into the other.

❂ Look through *The Way Things Work* by David Macaulay.

Pipe Cleaner Pilot

Pipe cleaners can bend and twist
and turn most every way,
Wind them into any shape
and that is how they stay!

Here's what you need

- Pipe cleaner
- Grocery tray from fruits or vegetables
- Construction paper scraps (dark blue)
- White craft glue
- Ballpoint pen
- Scissors

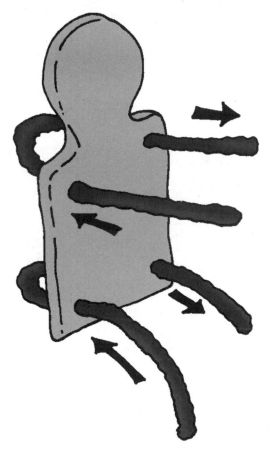

Here's what you do

❶ Cut out the head and body of the pilot from the center of the tray.

❷ Cut the pipe cleaner in half and put ends through body for pilot's arms and legs.

3 From blue construction paper, cut out front and back of shirt, pants, and hat. Tape onto pilot. Cut out eyes, mouth, and hair to glue onto pilot's face.

❂ Twist ends of pipe cleaner together for a bubble wand. Dip wand into a soap solution of $^1/_4$ cup (50 ml) dishwashing detergent and a small amount of water. Change the shape of the pipe cleaner to blow funny-shaped bubbles.

❂ Glue construction paper flowers to the tops of pipe cleaners. Place some clay or playdough in a paper cup; push in pipe cleaners for a paper plant.

FAST FACTS

In the flight deck of a jet liner, the captain sits on the left with the copilot on the right. At take-off they share the work, one steering and the other watching the instruments. The throttles controlling the engines are between them.

Yolk Folks

Eggs come by the dozen,
and can be eaten fried,
Use the shell for a face
when nothing's left inside!

Here's what you need

- Uncooked egg in shell
- Pin or small nail
- Thin straw
- Bowl
- Markers

Here's what you do

❶ Carefully twist the pin into the pointed end of the egg to make a small hole. Use the pin to make a larger hole at the other end of the egg. Insert straw in larger hole and blow the egg into the bowl.

❷ Rinse the eggshell in water and allow to dry. Gently draw a face on the shell with markers and decorate.

❸ Wash your hands in warm, soapy water after handling eggs.

IN THE BEGINNING

In the 1930s the average hen laid 121 eggs a year. Today a hen lays about 217 eggs a year.

NOW TRY THIS

◐ For a rainbow of people, dip the eggshells in food color mixed in water. Allow to dry before drawing on a face. Now put some yolk folks in your double-decker bus (page 28).

◐ Put a small amount of soil in half an eggshell. Plant a seed in the soil and stand the shell in the egg carton. Water seeds daily until they sprout.

On The Road

Vroom! Vroom!

Travel roads through hill and dale—
oh, zooming high and low.
It sure feels great when you drive
past places that you know!

Grocery Bag Tunnel

Driving through a tunnel,
day turns into night,
Then on the other side,
once again it's bright!

Here's what you need

- Large paper grocery bag
- Shirt cardboard
- Scissors
- Stapler

Here's what you do

1 Cut the grocery bag in half the long way. Open both halves; then lay one-half inside the other for a tunnel.

2 Fold up the edges all around and staple to hold in place.

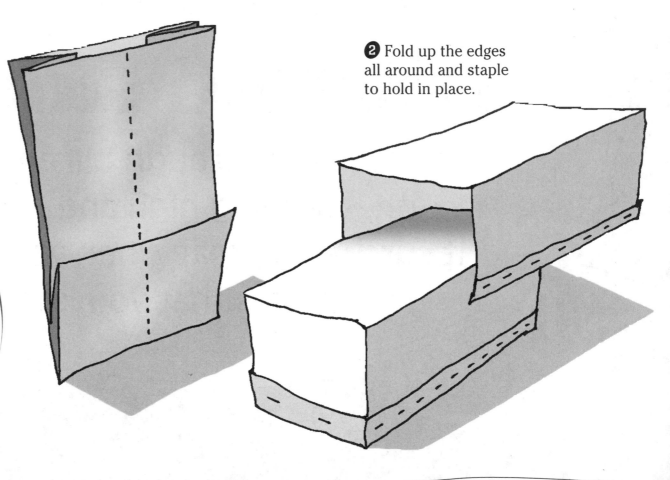

Curious Quotes

"Run for your lives, men!" said David Brown, construction foreman of the Holland Tunnel project between New York and New Jersey in 1924. He and his crew were digging 22 feet (6.6 meters) under the river bed when water gushed into the tunnel.

3 To make your tunnel sturdy, staple cardboard inside both ends of the tunnel. Then cut out openings for tunnel entrance and exit.

NOW TRY THIS

● Before constructing your tunnel, dip a sponge in brown or grey poster paint. Press onto the grocery bag. Allow to dry completely; then make the tunnel.

● Dip small pieces of natural sponge in green poster paint. Allow sponge to dry completely. Glue around sides of tunnel for plants.

Cereal Box Bridge

When crossing a river
that's long and very wide,
Build a bridge with boxes,
then walk to the other side!

Here's what you need

• Large cardboard cereal box
• Recycled aluminum foil
• Tape
• Scissors

Here's what you do

❶ Cut the cereal box in half the long way. Tape the ends of one half closed.

❷ Cut diagonally across both corners of one half-box. Cut up the short sides of the second half-box for flaps.

IN THE BEGINNING

*T*he Romans were the first great bridge builders, making bridges of wood that were so narrow only three men could cross at one time.

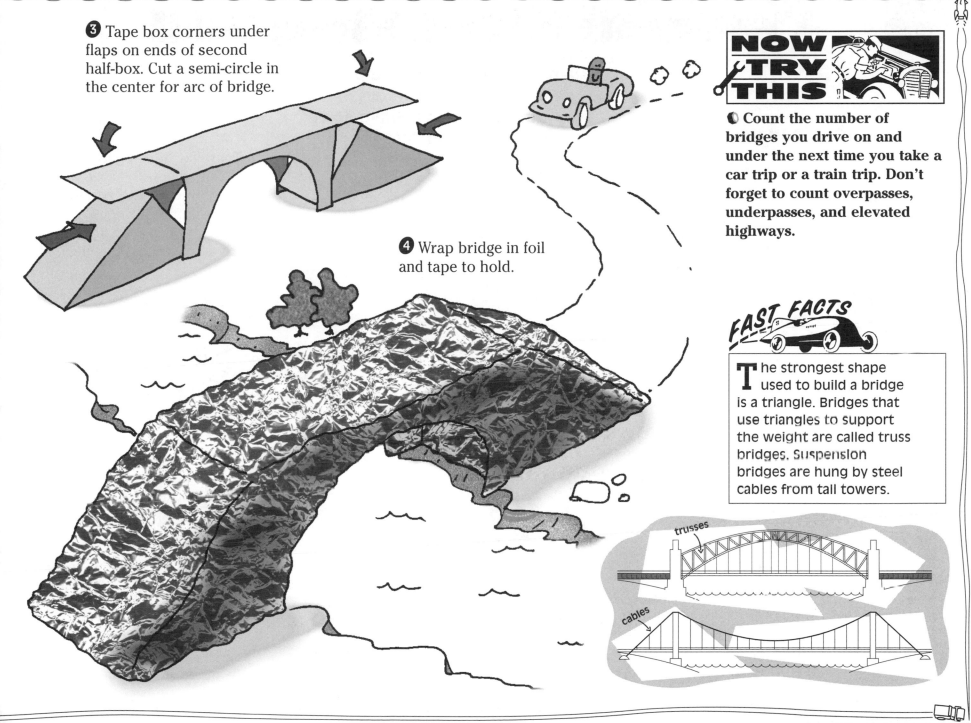

3 Tape box corners under flaps on ends of second half-box. Cut a semi-circle in the center for arc of bridge.

4 Wrap bridge in foil and tape to hold.

NOW TRY THIS

◖ Count the number of bridges you drive on and under the next time you take a car trip or a train trip. Don't forget to count overpasses, underpasses, and elevated highways.

FAST FACTS

The strongest shape used to build a bridge is a triangle. Bridges that use triangles to support the weight are called truss bridges. Suspension bridges are hung by steel cables from tall towers.

trusses

cables

Peanut Packing Hill

Use peanut packing from a box,
the kind that's used for fill,
Grab a bunch and glue them down
to build a peanut hill!

Here's what you need

- Peanut packing
- Tissue paper (green or brown)
- Paper bowl
- Shirt cardboard
- White craft glue
- Paintbrush
- Yogurt container

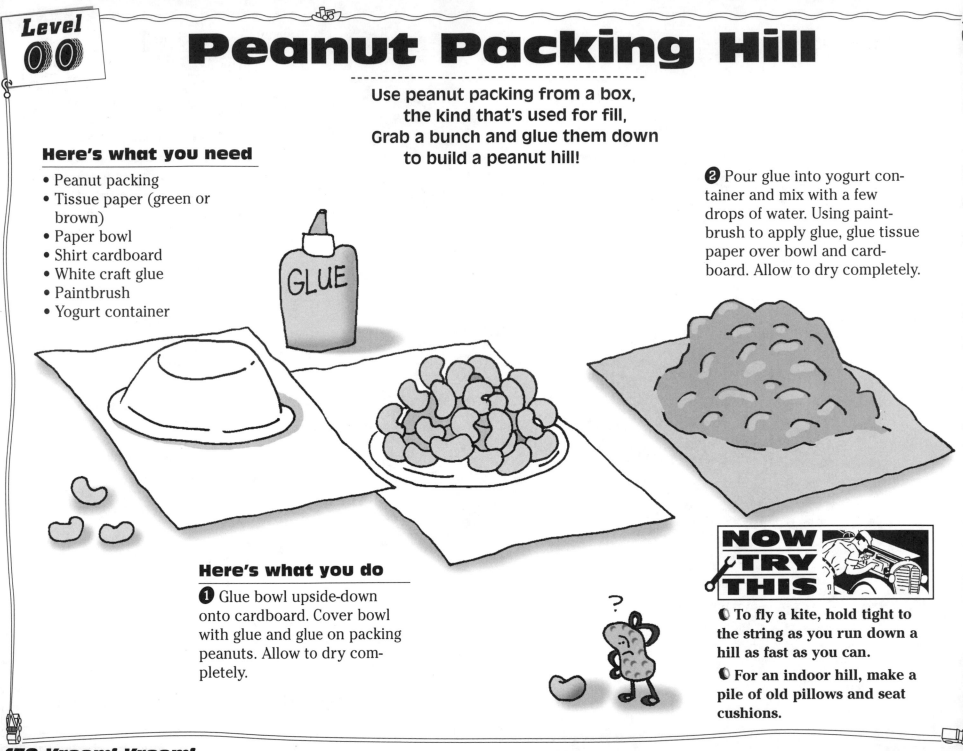

GLUE

❷ Pour glue into yogurt container and mix with a few drops of water. Using paintbrush to apply glue, glue tissue paper over bowl and cardboard. Allow to dry completely.

Here's what you do

❶ Glue bowl upside-down onto cardboard. Cover bowl with glue and glue on packing peanuts. Allow to dry completely.

NOW TRY THIS

◐ To fly a kite, hold tight to the string as you run down a hill as fast as you can.

◐ For an indoor hill, make a pile of old pillows and seat cushions.

Popsicle Stick Train Track

Popsicle sticks glued in a row
can make a great train track,
Here comes the train, it pulls the cars,
as wheels go clickety clack!

IN THE BEGINNING

The first rails were made of cast iron. These were strong enough to bear the weight of horse-drawn wagons, but the much heavier locomotives quickly cracked them.

Here's what you need

- Popsicle sticks
- 3 pieces heavy paper
- White craft glue
- Tape

Here's what you do

❶ Tape paper end to end for one long sheet. Glue down Popsicle sticks lengthwise to paper. Then cover with crosswise sticks for a train track.

Curious Quotes

"Gentlemen, with your assistance we will proceed to lay the last tie, the last rail, and drive the last spike." So said Leland Stanford, president of the Pacific Railroad, upon completion of the Transcontinental Railroad, May 10, 1869.

FAST FACTS

There is a ridge on the inside of train wheels that helps them stay on the rails.

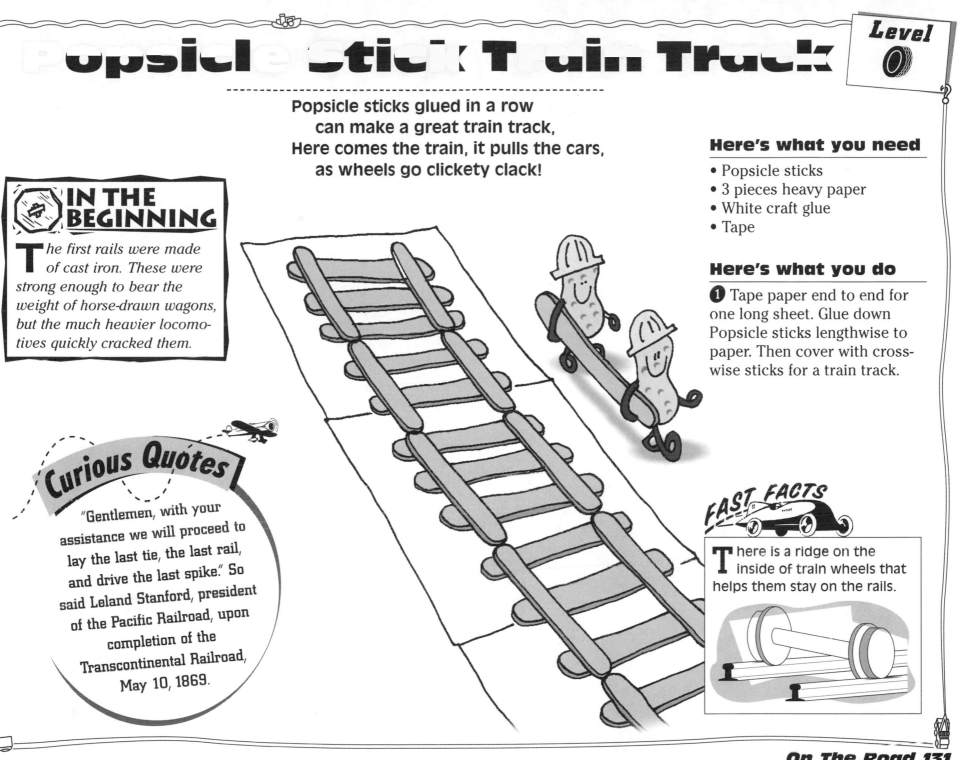

Paper Pine Trees

Walk into the forest,
to see where pine trees grow.
Some have grown very tall,
and some are short and low.

FAST FACTS

There are two main groups of trees, conifers (soft woods) and broadleaf trees (hardwoods). Most conifers carry their leaves (pine needles) all year. That is why they are called evergreens. Broadleaf trees in cooler climates are deciduous, which means they shed their leaves in the fall.

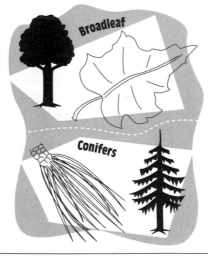

Broadleaf

Conifers

Here's what you need

• Construction paper (green)
• Popsicle sticks
• Cardboard egg carton
• White craft glue
• Scissors

Here's what you do

❶ Cut the egg carton in half. Cut out 2 sides of each tree at once from construction paper by folding paper over.

2 Glue trees onto both sides of Popsicle sticks. Turn egg carton upside-down, dip Popsicle sticks into glue, and then stick into sections of carton for a forest.

NOW TRY THIS

● Spread peanut butter over a pinecone; then roll it in bird-seed. Hang the pinecone in a tree to feed the birds in winter.

● Have you ever eaten pine nuts? Pignoli nuts are seeds that come from certain pine trees. Buy them in a grocery store and sprinkle on a plate of pasta for a tasty dish.

Paint Roller Road

Use a roller and black paint
to draw a road design,
Make it curve this way and that
and add a center line!

Here's what you need

- Large, empty thread spool
- Pipe cleaner
- Drinking straw
- Sponge
- Construction paper (black)
- White craft glue
- Poster paint (white or yellow)
- Heavy paper plate

Here's what you do

❶ Glue a thin piece of sponge to fit around the spool. (Hold sponge onto spool with a rubber band until it's dry.)

❷ Put pipe cleaner through center of spool. Twist ends together so spool rotates. Put pipe cleaner into straw for handle.

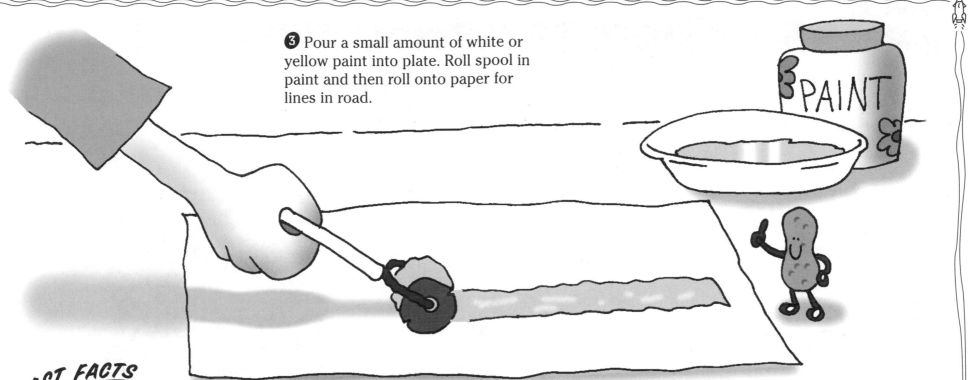

3 Pour a small amount of white or yellow paint into plate. Roll spool in paint and then roll onto paper for lines in road.

FAST FACTS

Interstate 80 goes all the way from New York City across the U.S.A. to San Francisco.

NOW TRY THIS

● Roll the roller in a straight line for roads that are straight. Curve it back and forth for a road that is curved. Use a long piece of butcher paper for a super highway.

● Cut a shirt cardboard in a diamond shape for a road sign. Use the roller to paint the curved lines and write CURVES AHEAD.

Toothpaste Box Gas Pump

Here's what you need

- Cardboard toothpaste box
- Recycled aluminum foil
- Construction paper scrap
- Tape
- Paper fastener
- Marker
- Thick black yarn
- Scissors

FAST FACTS

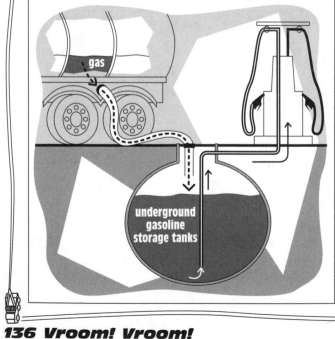

The gasoline at the gas station is stored in underground storage tanks.

gas

underground gasoline storage tanks

When the arrow points to empty,
you won't get very far,
Unless you pull up to the pump
and put gas in your car!

TOOTHPASTE

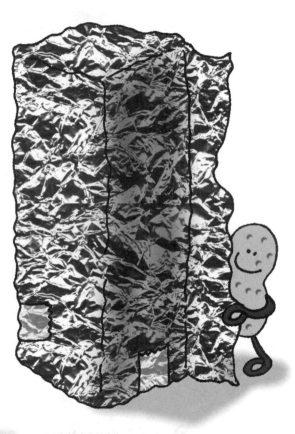

Here's what you do

❶ Cut away 2" (5 cm) from the open end of the toothpaste box. Wrap box in foil and tape to hold.

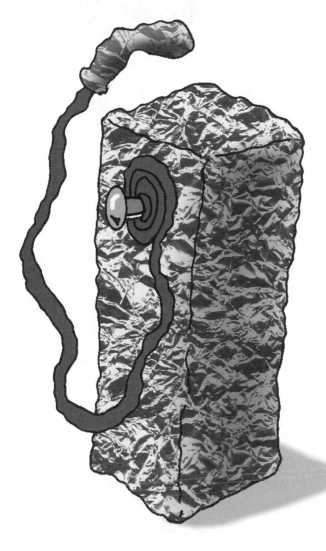

NOW TRY THIS

◐ **Fill a dishpan with soapy water and have a "car wash" for your plastic cars and trucks.**

◐ **When the air in your bicycle tires is low, visit a gas station to fill them up at the air pump.**

❸ Glue paper onto pump for a gas gauge.

❷ Attach paper fastener to side of box (spread prongs with head of fastener raised) and wrap yarn around for a hose. Wrap foil around end of yarn for a nozzle.

GAL.

$

Lunch Bag Buildings

Stuff brown paper lunch bags,
then turn them upside-down.
Draw windows, doors, and roofs,
to make a lunch bag town!

Here's what you need

- 3 paper lunch bags
- Newspaper
- White craft glue
- Markers
- Scissors

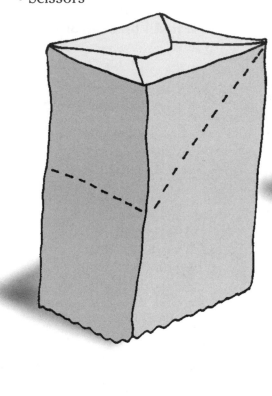

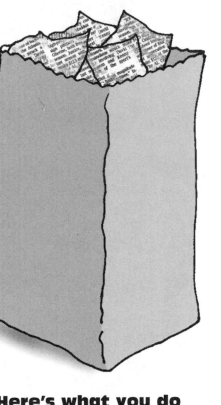

2 Turn the third bag upside down and use markers to draw doors, windows, plants, and a house number on the sides.

Here's what you do

1 Open wide the first lunch bag and then cut it diagonally across the bottom corner. Stuff the second bag partially full with crumpled newspaper.

3 Next, open the drawn-on bag and pull it down over the stuffed bag. Glue the corner of the first bag on top for a roof.

NOW TRY THIS

◐ Make a lunch bag building that looks like your home. Cut out faces from extra photographs and glue them in the windows.

◐ Look closely at the schools, places of worship, stores, and homes where you live. Use different-sized paper bags to make your town.

◐ Visit your town hall and ask to see the town plan. Notice which areas are commercial (stores), which are residential (homes), which are recreational (parks), and which are agricultural (farms).

Corrugated Cardboard Tree

A tree grows in the forest,
its trunk is straight and tall,
Leaves sprout in the springtime,
in autumn watch them fall!

Here's what you need

- Corrugated cardboard
- Construction paper (green)
- Shirt cardboard
- White craft glue
- Tape
- Scissors

FAST FACTS

The Macrozamia Tree, which grows in the Tambourine Mountains of Queensland, Australia, is estimated to be anywhere from 12,000 to 15,000 years old.

Here's what you do

❶ Peel back the smooth top sheet of paper from corrugated cardboard. Cut 2 rectangles wide enough to fold into a cylinder. Tape rectangle together for 2 cylinders.

❷ Cut slits in the base of one cylinder for tree trunk and cut long slits in the second cylinder for branches.

3 Spread apart slits of first cylinder and tape to cardboard base for a tree trunk. Put second cylinder into top of trunk for branches.

4 Glue construction paper leaves onto branches.

◖ Glue different construction paper leaves on the tree for each season. Use cotton or glitter for snow in winter.

◖ Compare the textures of bark on different trees, first by looking at them, then by touching them, and finally by doing bark rubbings.

◖ Have an outdoor picnic under a leafy tree. After eating, lie back and watch the leaves on the tree dancing in the breeze.

Recycled Foil Pond

If you want to make a pond,
some foil is your best bet.
Cut it out and glue it down,
then play as if it's wet!

Here's what you need

- Recycled aluminum foil
- Paper bowl
- Shirt cardboard
- Pom-pom or cotton ball
- White craft glue
- Markers
- Scissors

Here's what you do

1 Cut around the bottom of the bowl, leaving an edge all around. Wrap the bowl in foil for the pond.

2 Cut out the head and neck of a duck from the cardboard. Use markers to color both sides. Glue necks onto pom-pom or cotton ball and then glue ducks onto pond.

NOW TRY THIS

◑ Ducklings waddle in a row as they follow the mother duck. Use one large pom-pom for a mother duck and a row of small ones for the duck-lings. Then, read Robert McCloskey's *Make Way for Ducklings* — a treat for you or for a friend!

◑ Take a walk with a grown-up. Visit a pond and look for signs that critters have been along the edges. Watch tiny insects such as pond skaters and whirligig beetles walk on the pond's surface.

whirligig beetles

Vroom! Vroom!

Let's Play!

Some play days are indoors,
and some out in the sun.
Even if you play alone,
you still can have great fun.

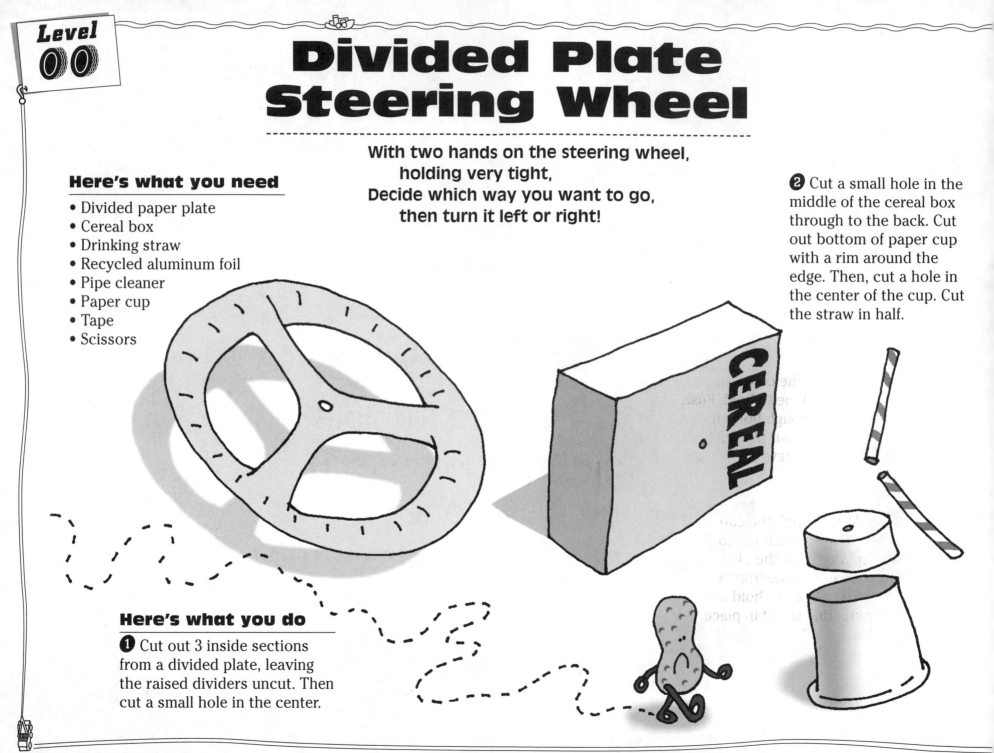

Divided Plate Steering Wheel

With two hands on the steering wheel,
holding very tight,
Decide which way you want to go,
then turn it left or right!

Here's what you need

- Divided paper plate
- Cereal box
- Drinking straw
- Recycled aluminum foil
- Pipe cleaner
- Paper cup
- Tape
- Scissors

Here's what you do

1 Cut out 3 inside sections from a divided plate, leaving the raised dividers uncut. Then cut a small hole in the center.

2 Cut a small hole in the middle of the cereal box through to the back. Cut out bottom of paper cup with a rim around the edge. Then, cut a hole in the center of the cup. Cut the straw in half.

NOW TRY THIS

● Tape your steering wheel inside a carton that's big enough to sit in. Tape wheels on the outside of the box and cut out the center of the front flap for a windshield. Take a passenger along for a ride.

❸ Wrap the cereal box in foil and tape to hold. Push straw through holes in box; then put pipe cleaner through straw.

❹ Sandwich the cup between the box and plate. Twist the pipe cleaner in the front and in the back to hold the steering wheel in place.

Shoe Box Garage

If a car has broken down
or tires need some air,
Garage mechanics fill up tanks
and know what to repair!

Here's what you need

- Cardboard shoe box (with lid)
- White craft glue
- Markers
- Tape
- Scissors

Here's what you do

❶ Cut away the front panel of the shoe box. Then cut along the edges of the bottom of the box for a flap. Cut out a rectangle in the center of the flap; cut the rectangle in half horizontally.

NOW TRY THIS

◐ Use toy cars and trucks in your garage and put them up on the lift.

◐ If you are really interested in cars, read *Car Care For Kids And Former Kids* by Harvey G. Lord to learn more about car repair.

❸ Cut edge of shoe-box lid so it is flat. Use markers to draw shelves and tools.

❷ Turn the box upside-down on its lid and tape the rectangle halves to both sides of flap so roof of garage is curved.

Towel Tube Road Sign

Road signs tell you everything
a driver needs to know:
School Crossing, Sharp Curves Ahead,
Use Caution, and Go Slow!

Here's what you need

- Construction paper (red, orange, white, black)
- Cardboard paper towel tube
- White craft glue
- Tape
- Scissors

Here's what you do

❶ Cut black and red paper in a circle. Then cut the letters S T O P from the white paper, and S L O W from the black paper. Cut a diamond shape from the orange paper.

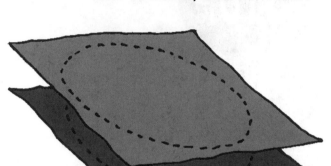

STOP
SLOW

❷ Glue S T O P on red circle and S L O W on orange diamond. Glue diamond onto black circle. Glue circles back to back.

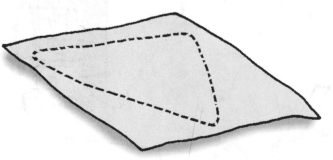

ORANGE

BLACK

RED

3 Cut a slit in the top of the tube. Tape circles into slit in tube for a road sign.

Road signs are color-coded: red signs prohibit movement (STOP); yellow are warning signs (curve in road); white are regulatory signs (no parking); and green are guide signs (exit signs).

STOP

STOP

SLOW

Ice Cream Store Ahead

NOW TRY THIS

◑ **Make up your own road signs.** Some ideas are "Ice-Cream Store Ahead," "Caution: Zoo Animals," "Library Crossing," and "Circus Coming To Town."

Cardboard Carton Plane

Step aboard a carton plane
to get from here to there,
Though this plane stays on the ground,
it takes you everywhere!

Here's what you need

- Large cardboard carton
- Recycled aluminum foil
- Shirt cardboard
- Paper fastener
- Packing tape
- Scissors

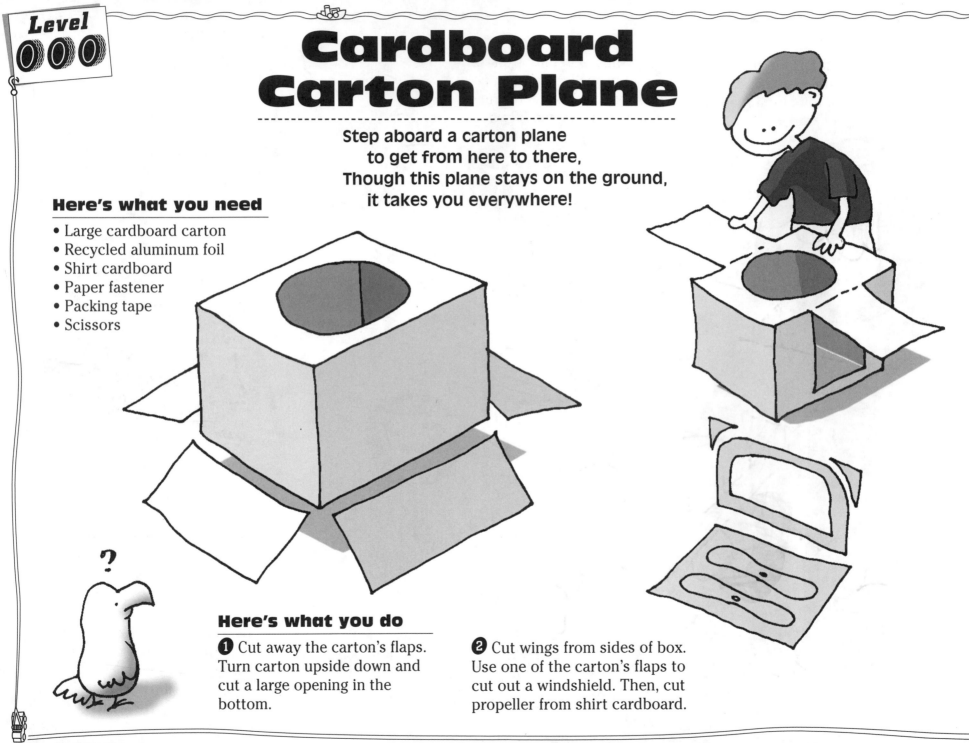

Here's what you do

❶ Cut away the carton's flaps. Turn carton upside down and cut a large opening in the bottom.

❷ Cut wings from sides of box. Use one of the carton's flaps to cut out a windshield. Then, cut propeller from shirt cardboard.

3 Tape windshield onto front of box. Wrap propeller in foil and attach to box with fastener. Put plane on over head and lift your arms to spread plane's wings.

NOW TRY THIS

🖤 Design a logo (symbol) for your own airline and then paint it on the side of your carton plane.

🖤 Celebrate a special occasion with a travel party. Send out invitations in the shape of an airplane and ask each guest to wear a costume according to their destination.

🖤 Read *Sally Ride: Shooting for the Stars* by Jane Hurwitz for an exciting story about astronauts.

Cereal Box Suitcase

Get ready to go on a trip,
be sure that you don't rush,
Pack everything that you may need,
including your toothbrush!

Here's what you need

- Medium-size cereal box
- Shirt cardboard
- Wide ribbon
- Gift wrap paper
- 2 paper fasteners
- Tape
- Scissors

Here's what you do

❶ Cut around 3 sides of the front panel of the cereal box. Cut 2 slits in the side of the box.

❷ Cut out a handle from shirt cardboard. Cut 2 pieces of ribbon long enough to wrap around the box.

3 Wrap box and handle in gift wrap (wrap top flap separately to open and close) for suitcase. Tape to hold.

4 Wrap ribbons around suitcases and hold in place with fasteners. Put ends of handle in slits cut in top of suitcase and tape to hold.

Patty
123 MAIN ST.
VERMONT, NH
555-1212

Jim

NOW TRY THIS

◐ Make luggage tags for your suitcase with your name, address, and phone number. Be sure to include the country you live in.

◐ Pack the suitcase with special things you'll want to take with you on a trip (don't forget your toothbrush!).

◐ Before you take your next trip, pack up a bag of the following treats: snacks to munch on, crayons and paper, stickers, and a favorite book to read.

Milk Carton Traffic Light

Drivers watch the traffic light,
the bottom light is green,
Red is at the very top,
and yellow's in-between!

Here's what you need

- Quart (946 ml) milk carton
- Construction paper (black, red, yellow, green)
- String
- Tape
- White craft glue
- Scissors

Here's what you do

❶ Rinse, dry, and open spout on milk carton. Tape spout flaps closed. Cut a hole through the spout.

HOLE

❷ Cut a circle from red, green, and yellow construction paper; then cut 3 long, thin rectangles from black paper.

3 Wrap carton in black construction paper and tape to hold. Glue circles onto carton for traffic light and tape rectangles above. Put thread through hole to hang light.

Frost 3 cupcakes with icing tinted red, yellow, and green, for a tasty "traffic light" snack.

Four-sided traffic lights, run automatically by an electric timer and are programmed to keep traffic running smoothly.

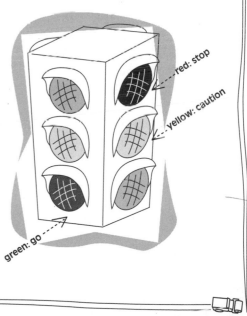

red: stop

yellow: caution

green: go

Index

Kids Can!

The following *Kids Can!*® books for ages 4 to 12 are each 160-176 pages, fully illustrated, trade paper, 11 x 8 ½, $12.95 US.

CUT-PAPER PLAY!
Dazzling Creations from Construction Paper
by Sandi Henry

American Bookseller Pick of the List
SUPER SCIENCE CONCOCTIONS
50 Mysterious Mixtures for Fabulous Fun
by Jill Frankel Hauser

MAKING COOL CRAFTS & AWESOME ART
A Treasure Trove of Fabulous Fun
by Roberta Gould

HAND-PRINT ANIMAL ART
by Carolyn Carreiro

Parents' Choice Gold Award
Parents Magazine Parents' Pick
THE KIDS' NATURE BOOK
365 Indoor/Outdoor Activities and Experiences
by Susan Milord

Parents' Choice Approved
Benjamin Franklin Best Multicultural Book Award
Skipping Stones Multicultural Honor Award
THE KIDS' MULTICULTURAL COOKBOOK
Food & Fun Around the World
by Deanna F. Cook

KIDS' COMPUTER CREATIONS
Using Your Computer for Art & Craft Fun
by Carol Sabbeth

Parents' Choice Approved
Dr. Toy's Best Vacation Product Award
KIDS GARDEN!
The Anytime, Anyplace Guide to Sowing & Growing Fun
by Avery Hart and Paul Mantell

Benjamin Franklin Science/Educational Book Award
Winner of the Oppenheim Toy Portfolio Best Book Award
American Bookseller Pick of the Lists
THE KIDS' SCIENCE BOOK
Creative Experiences for Hands-On Fun
by Robert Hirschfeld and Nancy White

Parents' Choice Gold Award
American Bookseller Pick of the Lists
Winner of the Oppenheim Toy Portfolio Best Book Award
THE KIDS' MULTICULTURAL ART BOOK
Art & Craft Experiences from Around the World
by Alexandra M. Terzian

Parents' Choice Gold Award
Benjamin Franklin Best Juvenile Nonfiction Award
KIDS MAKE MUSIC!
Clapping and Tapping from Bach to Rock
by Avery Hart and Paul Mantell

KIDS & WEEKENDS!
Creative Ways to Make Special Days
by Avery Hart and Paul Mantell

Dr. Toy's Best Vacation Product Award
American Bookseller Pick of the Lists
KIDS' CRAZY CONCOCTIONS
50 Mysterious Mixtures for Art & Craft Fun
by Jill Frankel Hauser

Winner of the Oppenheim Toy Portfolio Best Book Award
Skipping Stones Nature & Ecology Honor Award
EcoArt!
Earth-Friendly Art & Craft Experiences for 3- to 9-Year-Olds
by Laurie Carlson

KIDS COOK!
Fabulous Food for the Whole Family
by Sarah Williamson and Zachary Williamson

THE KIDS' WILDLIFE BOOK
Exploring Animal Worlds through Indoor/Outdoor
Crafts & Experiences
by Warner Shedd

HANDS AROUND THE WORLD
365 Creative Ways to Build Cultural Awareness &
Global Respect
by Susan Milord

KIDS CREATE!
Art & Craft Experiences for 3- to 9-Year-Olds
by Laurie Carlson

Parents Magazine Parents' Pick
KIDS LEARN AMERICA!
Bringing Geography to Life with People, Places, & History
by Patricia Gordon and Reed C. Snow

American Bookseller Pick of the Lists
ADVENTURES IN ART
Art & Craft Experiences for 7- to 14-Year-Olds
by Susan Milord

Little Hands

The following *Little Hands*™ books for ages 2 to 6 are each 144 pages, fully illustrated, trade paper, 10 x 8, $12.95 US.

Children's Book-of-the-Month Main Selection
THE LITTLE HANDS ART BOOK
Exploring Arts & Crafts with 2- to 6-Year-Olds
by Judy Press

Parents' Choice Approved
The Little Hands BIG FUN CRAFT Book
Creative Fun for 2- to 6-Year-Olds
by Judy Press

American Bookseller Pick of the List
RAINY DAY PLAY!
Explore, Create, Discover, Pretend
by Nancy Fusco Castaldo

STOP, LOOK & LISTEN!
Using Your Senses from Head to Toe
by Sarah A. Williamson

Parents' Choice Approved
1997 Director's Choice Award from Early Childhood Education
SHAPES, SIZES, & MORE SURPRISES!
A Little Hands Early Learning Book
by Mary Tomczyk

Parents' Choice Approved
SUNNY DAYS & STARRY NIGHTS
A Little Hands Nature Book
by Nancy Fusco Castaldo

MATH PLAY!
80 Ways to Count & Learn
by Mark Schrooten and Diane McGowan

More Books from Williamson Publishing!

Parents' Choice Honor Award
Stepping Stones Multicultural Honor Award
Benjamin Franklin Best Juvenile Fiction Award
TALES ALIVE!
Ten Multicultural Folktales with Activities
by Susan Milord
128 pages, 8 ½ x ll, four-color original
illustrations, $15.95

Parents' Choice Approved
TALES OF THE SHIMMERING SKY
Ten Global Folktales with Activities
by Susan Milord
128 pages, 8 ½ x 11, four-color original illustrations,
$15.95

PYRAMIDS!
50 hands-on activities to experience ancient Egypt
by Avery Hart and Paul Mantell
96 pages, 10 x 10, two-color original illustrations,
$9.95

To see what's new at Williamson and learn more about specific books, visit our website at:

http://www.williamsonbooks.com

To Order Books from Williamson Publishing directly:

You'll find Williamson Books at your favorite bookstore. Or, order directly from Williamson Publishing. We accept Visa and MasterCard (please include the number and expiration date), or send check to:

Williamson Publishing Company
Church Hill Road, P.O. Box 185
Charlotte, Vermont 05445

Toll-free phone orders with credit cards:
1-800-234-8791

E-mail orders with credit cards:
order@williamsonbooks.com

Catalog request: mail, phone, or e-mail to given addresses.

Please add **$3.00** for postage for one book plus **50 cents** for each additional book. Satisfaction is guaranteed or full refund without questions or quibbles.

Prices may be slightly higher when purchased in Canada.

Kids Can!®, *Little Hands*®, *Tales Alive*®, and *Kaleidoscope Kids*® are registered trademarks of Williamson Publishing.